The Ultimate Guide to
Buying and Selling Homes

Insights from America's
Top Agents

David Worters

Mike Deck

Matt Bauscher

Cheryl and Brad Fuqua

Michelle Noble

Paul George

Scott Oyler

Tonya Marlatt

Jon Holsten

Kim Ziton

Table of Contents

Introduction

According to the National Association of REALTORS® there are over 1.3 million real estate agent or broker members in the United States. The publisher selected ten top real estate agents and brokers from around the county to contribute to this book. Mortgage lenders are a critical component of most real estate transactions. The publisher selected a top mortgage company branch manager and loan officer to contribute to the book to describe lending strategies for successful real estate transactions.

Each of the contributors has a high volume of completed transactions, is highly rated by their clients, and is an advocate for their clients' success. The contributors are spread out geographically across the United States. Each contributor has provided their insights for home buyers and/or sellers in their respective area and with strategies that can work anywhere in the country. We hope that this book will become a useful reference for consumers interested in buying or selling homes around the United States.

NMG Publishing

Buying or Selling a Home in Fast-Moving Markets

David Worters

Introduction

After a twenty-year career in the performing arts, managing symphony orchestras, David Worters decided to pursue a career in an independent and entrepreneurial field where his people-oriented personality would be an asset. He decided to enter the real estate field and has enjoyed success helping buyers and sellers in North Carolina's Triangle region ever since. David is affiliated with Hodge & Kittrell Sotheby's in Raleigh and has consistently been a top producer with the firm, selling more homes than any other agent over the past five years. He has also won several awards for excellence in real estate sales.

David focuses his real estate practice on Wake County including the cities of Raleigh, Cary, Morrisville, Apex and the surrounding areas. He works with experienced buyers and sellers and enjoys working with first-time homebuyers.

In this chapter David provides insights for buyers and sellers in fast-moving markets.

Buying Your Home

Regardless of whether it's a first-time purchase or you're an experienced buyer, purchasing a home is one of the biggest financial transactions of a lifetime. It's often happening at a time of other stressful events in life, like a birth, a death, a new job, a loss of a job, a marriage or a divorce. Buying a home will have significant implications for your finances for the long term. When you are planning on purchasing a home, start with an understanding of the price range that is going to make you happy. It doesn't make sense to go shopping at one price level and to get excited about a home, only to then go seek financing and find out what the monthly payment is going to look like, or that you can't qualify for a loan at that level. Getting all the facts is important as you may also find out that you can comfortably afford a higher-priced home than you had been considering.

You should start by meeting with a mortgage loan officer who can explain the various options for fixed and adjustable rates, along with different down payment scenarios to figure out your home price range sweet spot. Part of this process involves getting pre-approved for financing so that you can demonstrate to sellers and their agents that you have the mortgage-worthiness to close on a loan. Today's reality is that offers are very rarely considered without strong evidence of mortgage pre-approval. If you're out house hunting, and your dream home pops up, it's the wrong time to start building your file with a loan officer because you'll be competing against people who have already been approved. I can recommend loan officers that have an excellent track record in helping with pre-approval as well as can get mortgages closed on time.

Most people looking for a home today start their search online. Since most homes for sale can be found online, some people think all you need to do is to contact listing agents to view the homes and then work directly with the listing agent when you identify your ideal home. Although this is possible, remember that the listing agent is working for the seller and is looking out for the seller's interests, not yours. If you enter the home buying process without your own agent, who is going to advocate for your best interests? It's like walking into a courtroom without a lawyer, and if you try to do it on your own, then you're at a distinct disadvantage. An experienced buyer's agent can provide the advice, insight, wisdom and guidance to help a you make the best decision on a home purchase as well as guiding you through the negotiations and process to a successful closing. You'll be best served by having someone who is there to advocate for your interests and only your interests. When guiding buyers, part of my role involves helping with understanding of what a home is worth and an independent evaluation of the positives and downsides. Sometimes my role even involves trying to put the brakes on a buyer, so they don't make a major mistake with a purchase.

With so much relocation into the greater Raleigh area, also known as the Triangle, many of our buyers are moving into the area for the first time. It's a large geographic area that accommodates a wide variety of lifestyles, so narrowing down the location helps focus on homes that may be the best fit. What kind of experience and lifestyle are you looking for? What do you like to do when you're not at home? Is proximity to restaurants, cultural venues, professional or college sports or outdoor activities important to you? Raleigh, Durham, and Chapel Hill all provide an urban living experience, but each city provides a different and unique experience. There are beautiful suburban areas and even more rural communities near the cities. Job location and commuting expectations are also important factors for most people.

Try to make a list of things that you absolutely need in a new home and another list of things that you want. Once we get an understanding of these preferences, we can focus on specific locations and neighborhoods. Sometimes we need to drive around the area, getting to know the community, and discover what different neighborhoods offer.

As a newcomer to the area, it can be difficult to immediately decide on a specific community and go straight into home ownership. There's much to be said for taking a pause, getting a short-term rental, and getting to know the community before buying a home.

As you are actively looking at houses, remember that there is no such thing as the perfect home. Your list of needs and wants can help sort out the homes that best match your requirements, but in the end it's not likely that every desire will be met, unless you have the funds to build a custom home that includes everything you want.

After you have been looking at several homes, you will start to get a better idea of how prices compare and start to visualize the value. Of course, as a buyer's agent I'll help you evaluate the fair market price of a home that you want to purchase, just as if I were working with a seller. It's important to keep in mind that the list price is not necessarily the market value. It may have been priced high or low compared to the market. Sometimes a seller intentionally, or just ill-advisedly, lists the home too low. Most likely in this case the home will attract multiple offers, and they may go far over asking price. You don't want to be the one buyer sitting there just offering the asking price, because of a philosophical stance against offering more that the list price in such case.

A lot of people think they should evaluate the price in terms of dollars per square foot, but this is just a trap. If two homes in the neighborhood sold for $270 per square foot, it's easy to think you shouldn't pay more than that for another home in the neighborhood. That's not generally going to get you the correct value of the home, because there are far too many things that make a home unique including the lot, the specific location, the upgrades, the floor plan, the topography of the land, the condition and other factors. One possible exception here may be with condominiums in a high-rise building, where price per foot can be a useful tool, because the units are so similar. But with respect to single family homes, I'd rather not even talk about price per foot, because it just misses too much in terms of value.

With the market we have been experiencing, once we have done the hard work of looking at a lot of houses, and really understanding what we're looking for, it's critical to move fast when you see the one you want. The most attractive homes will sell quickly, so you really need to get into "pounce mode," because other buyers are seeing the same homes you are seeing hit the market. When a new listing that looks right for you pops up, it's best to visit it the first day on the market and be able to make a quick decision. In a tight market, time is not on our side and too many buyers make the mistake of not listening to their instincts, sleeping on it, only to wake up in the morning with an alert from a website indicating that the house they just looked at went under contract the prior night. Sadly, many buyers learn that lesson the hard way. It's not the end of the world; there will always be another house. But I just hate to watch that heartbreak firsthand.

Most people moving within the area are selling their existing home and buying a new home. This is a complex maneuver and I suggest that you carefully consider the options available to simultaneously buy and sell a home. There are three typical paths that can be taken. In my mind there's the easy path, the scary path and the difficult path.

The easiest path, which is also the safest path, requires the most logistics. The first step is to sell your existing home. Then you move into a short-term rental, and then purchase something when you find that home you really like. This process is easier because you don't have to own two homes at once. This path also takes all the pressure off rigid timelines on either the buying or selling side. Although it relieves the pressure, it introduces an additional move and there's the hassle of a short-term rental. You will enjoy the experience much more when you are selling, because you will never be under any pressure to sell in a certain timeframe and likewise you can afford to sit back and wait for your perfect house, or your almost perfect house.

The scariest path, and usually the most difficult route financially, is to find your new home first and close on that home. After finding your new home you put your existing home up for sale. This can be scary because it involves owning two homes at once, and sometimes that is financially impossible. But even when it's possible, it can be stressful and scary if the old house does not sell quickly.

The difficult path entails finding the home you want to buy first and getting it under contract. As soon as you have the new home under contract, then you list your existing home and try to get it to sell quickly and to close one day before the closing on your new home. Although theoretically possible, it's difficult to pull this off because everything falls down like a house of cards if you cannot get your existing house to sell as quickly as you need it to.

A home is an important part of everyone's financial foundation and finding and purchasing the right home takes careful consideration. An experienced buyer's agent can help you identify the locations and neighborhoods that best match your requirements, guide you all the way through the process and help you negotiate the best price and terms for your new home.

Selling Your Home

When you are considering selling your home, it's important to have your expectations aligned with your real estate agent. It's easy to have a misunderstanding on things like the value, pricing strategy and the estimated time to sell your home. Although some agents may tell you what you want to hear, you're not being well served unless your agent does a thorough analysis of your home and provides independent insight on estimated selling price and how long it's going to take to sell. There's a real trap in sellers thinking that the best agent for them is the one who gives them the highest number.

One of the first topics that arises when I meet with someone that is interested in selling their home is, "How much is my home worth?" There are several online sites that provides estimates of value, and most people planning on selling their home have looked at the online value estimates. Unfortunately, these online value estimates are a distraction and unhelpful. They are based on a computer algorithm that uses raw statistical data to compare homes. The algorithm has not been in your home, nor any of the other homes used as a base of comparison. Critical factors, like the condition, quality of construction, level of upgrades and finishes, the view, and many other important differences are not known by the computer. These estimates can be either way too high or way too low, but they are rarely accurate. Also, tax values are not relevant when estimating market value.

The only real determination of value is what a buyer is willing to pay. It takes an experienced agent to accurately estimate the market value. That's not something I, or any other agent for that matter, can make an accurate estimate of until visiting the property and seeing all that it has to offer. After walking through the home for maybe an hour, I have enough information to understand all the features and possible weaknesses of the home. Then I can do the research on recent comparable homes that have sold and make comparisons to your home to come up with a market value estimate.

After we've determined the estimated market value for your home, how should the list price be determined? Some people believe that a home should be listed well above the market value because they think that buyers are going to try to negotiate a big reduction in the price anyway, so pricing it higher will allow room for negotiations, and the price can be reduced later. The reality is that many ideal buyers are going to pass on even taking a serious look at the home if it's priced too high. I tend to recommend a list price that is just a very small amount above what I believe is the actual market value. The most activity is generally just after the home is listed, so we want to create excitement and urgency among buyers when the home is first on the market. That will cause a lot of showings right up front, and hopefully competition to buy the home.

If you aim too high, you're going to wind up with a worse result than if you'd just priced it right the first time around.

With little activity and no serious offers, you are forced into a price reduction, or maybe even a series of reductions, and the home is going to sell for less than if it had been priced right the first time. The listing gets stale. People looking at the listing wonder what's wrong with the home since the listing has lingered on the market and the price has gone through a series of reductions. The value of your home is dropping every day that it's on the market. It's worth the most on the very first day that it hits the market.

Markets change based on several factors, including the national and local economy, interest rates, and most importantly the local balance in supply and demand. The Raleigh area has been experiencing incredible growth - there are between 60 and 70 people a day moving to this community. People moving to the area from almost any other metro area in the country feel like the housing in Raleigh is very affordable. The problem is that there are far more buyers than there are quality homes for sale, just not enough housing inventory. So most of the properly priced and presented homes sell very rapidly. But that doesn't mean all homes will sell quickly, even in a strong market. Less attractive homes or homes that have a particular issue or flaw will generally take longer to sell. Concerns like the lot being under a power line, having a steep driveway, or being on a busy road make the property less attractive and it may take longer to find the right buyer who doesn't mind the issue. It's better for the seller to clearly understand the expectations up front on how long it is going to take to sell.

I'm not a big proponent of suggesting that you make a lot of changes to your home before you sell. Although some agents might come in and say you should put in hardwood floors or remodel the kitchen, these are big expense items and not usually necessary. Primarily, the home needs to be clean and organized. A good example is what the showrooms looks like in a Pottery Barn or Restoration Hardware store. Everything looks neat and pretty, without a lot of clutter.

Much of the real estate business is now driven by digital online marketing and the pictures and other information seen online now gives the first impression for most people looking at your home. As we are getting ready to market your home, the most important day in the entire process is the photo shoot day. That's the day that you want to put your best foot forward. For that one day I recommend putting away most of the knick-knacks. Neaten up shelving and counters and put away most of the kitchen gadgets. Have everything as pristine as possible. I also suggest adding some fresh flowers for some nice color that will look great in the pictures.

High-quality, professional photos are critical to showing your home to its maximum advantage. I use a professional photographer who composes the pictures to show the home in the best lighting and from angles that make the spaces appear as generous as possible. It's important to focus on the best features and on rooms and areas where people will be spending their time. The kitchen is always one of the most important rooms, as well as the master bedroom and bath. If you have an outdoor living space, that's important to show because it's an area where people can imagine spending their leisure time.

Once the photography is completed, go back to living your life. We don't want your home to look sterile or fake. It should look like somebody lives there.

With most people starting their home search online, we need to make sure that our listing is seen by as many potential buyers as possible. My listings are syndicated to many consumer real estate sites, like Zillow and Trulia, where people are looking for homes. A listing should show up as high as possible in the order shown to potential buyers to attract the maximum attention. I invest in premium listings on these sites, so they will show up at the very top when buyers are searching.

Another point that I consider important is to have the online inquires come directly to me, instead of other random agents. I know more about my listings than any other agent and I want to make sure that potential buyers get firsthand information on all the great features and benefits and motivate them to see the home in person. My agency, Sotheby's International Realty, has exclusive partnerships with the Wall Street Journal, New York

Times, and Financial Times. We can expose our listings through these online publications to people who are thinking about the possibility of buying a house in places where they are in their everyday lives.

Neighbors are a good source of leads because they may have friends or relatives interested in buying a home in the neighborhood. They may not always realize your home is for sale if they are not driving by or looking at real estate sites. I typically conduct a neighborhood-based direct mail campaign just as the home is coming to market to get the word out and create some buzz around the listing.

In the tight market we have been experiencing, you're going to learn very quickly the market's response to your home. In a hot market, with limited inventory, if you don't have an offer in the first week, you are already becoming a stale listing. In that scenario, where you've been on the market a week or two and then you get an offer, you should pay attention, because your first offer is usually your best offer. It's best to take that first offer very seriously and make your best effort to get it worked out.

Feedback from the market will confirm how well your home is positioned against other competing homes. I try to get feedback after each showing to see what the potential buyers liked and didn't like about the home and how it compares. If we're not getting offers, we generally don't hear that price is the issue. There's a pretty big misconception that if we aren't getting comments about the price, then the price isn't the issue. The fact is that it's almost always about the price if your home is not getting sold, so we may need to go back and reassess the pricing.

On the other hand, if you are in a situation where you are clearly going to receive multiple offers, it makes much more sense to relax and give careful consideration before accepting an offer. The buyers aren't going to take their offers off the table. In this case it's better to give your home two, three or four days of exposure so that you can have as many offers as possible to select among. Remember that the highest price offer is not always the *best* offer. We want to select a buyer who has the ability to close, so it's also about their financing and the deposit. You learn a lot about the buyer's interest by the magnitude of the deposit that they're offering.

Even in the best of market conditions, selling a home is a complex process and an experienced real estate agent can help you realize the maximum price and profit upon sale.

Selecting an Agent to Help You Buy or Sell Your Home

A home is one of a family's or an individual's largest financial assets and buying or selling a home is an emotional experience. Selecting the right real estate agent to guide you through the process can make a big difference in your outcome and in the level of stress you will feel. It's important to select someone whom you believe you can trust that will be working on your behalf, even when you are not together. Time is of the essence in real estate transactions, so your agent should give you the feeling that they will be responsive and available.

Sometimes trusted friends or relatives can recommend an agent that has served them well, but I'd recommend interviewing a few agents before making a selection. It seems intuitive that sellers would interview multiple agents before choosing, but it doesn't seem so intuitive for buyers, even though the financial stakes are similar. Online reviews are easy to find, and you can get some indications of how well clients have been served by looking at the reviews. You can also ask for and check client references.

Experience in real estate is developed over several years and with volume of successful transactions. As you are doing your research, look at the agent's list of completed transactions to see if it represents the level of experience you are expecting. Sales award achievements are another indicator of success. If you are selling your home, inquire how your home will be marketed. Ask to look at examples of recent marketing campaigns used for sold listings. Does the agent do enough volume to be able to spend on marketing?

What Clients Are Saying

"David worked tirelessly to provide us with the information we needed to help make a decision to move in the first place and, later where exactly to settle here locally. Even though we weren't certain of many of our decisions, David never put pressure on us. He simply wanted to provide us with everything we could ever possibly need to be informed. David went to incredible lengths for us throughout the process, as if everything we asked for was his top priority. He became a friend while he was working hard to land us in a home that would best suit us. David's extensive knowledge of the area, its homes, and the who's who helped us in the negotiation process as well as in broader views on neighborhoods, school, work commutes, etc. We ended up in our dream home and managed to do so quite painlessly with him by our side. We honestly couldn't have done it without him."

—Maggie and Mike (Raleigh)

"David could not have done a better job for us! He went above and beyond in every regard, and his professionalism and attention to detail were only surpassed by his integrity, patience and kindness. We feel so fortunate that David was the first realtor our daughter met when she began the search for a house in Raleigh. He was quick to respond to every question; readily available to show properties as soon as they became available; very knowledgeable about neighborhoods, relative values, legalities, etc., and he anticipated every step ahead of us throughout the process. He advised, guided, encouraged, and reassured, and was always upbeat and willing to help us with anything

and everything from start to finish. We could not have asked for a finer or more diligent realtor, or a greater overall experience."

—Claire and Jeff (Raleigh)

"If you are looking for a valued partner to help you in purchasing a home, look no further. David is extremely competent, hard working, and an absolute pleasure to work with. I could not imagine working with another realtor...he turned what could have been a very difficult and laborious process into a wonderful experience. I value excellent service and David surpassed every expectation. There are many choices to make in life and choosing to work with David was a choice I'd make again and again."

—Alison and Matthew (Cary)

"David was the best real estate agent we have ever worked with. We just finished working with David to buy our new home and sell our existing home. He guided us correctly through every step. He demonstrates true understanding of the market, the science of the process and the art of negotiation. All of his advise and recommendations were spot on correct. He was always available 24/7, and answered our questions before we even asked them."

—Suzanne and Bill (Raleigh)

About David Worters

David Worters's real estate practice is based in Raleigh, North Carolina. He is consistently one of the top producers within Hodge & Kittrell Sotheby's International Realty and works with both buyers and sellers. David is in the Triangle Business Journal's "Book of Lists" as one of the "Top Real Estate Agents in the Tringle" and REAL Trends also named him to the "Top Agents in America" list. His real estate career has been profiled by both the News & Observer and the Triangle Business Journal, and he is a frequent source for news stories concerning real estate as it relates to the public school assignment system in Wake County. The News & Observer honored David's contributions to North Carolina when it named him "Tar Heel of the Week" in 2010.

A longtime resident of Raleigh and customer of the firm, David choose Hodge & Kittrell Sotheby's International Realty after a twenty-year career in the performing arts. As President & CEO of the North Carolina Symphony for more than a decade, he oversaw the Symphony's role in the opening of Meymandi Concert Hall in downtown Raleigh and the outdoor Koka Booth Amphitheatre at Regency Park in Cary, as well as the introduction of Grant Llewellyn as the Symphony's fifth music director. Prior to relocating to Raleigh and making it his permanent home in the late 1990s, David resided in Boston, MA; Fort Worth, TX; Syracuse, NY; Chicago, IL; Spokane, WA; and San Francisco, CA.

David grew up in Newton, Massachusetts, just outside of Boston. He earned his undergraduate degree in economics at Harvard. He is married to Miranda Yeager, an executive in the health care industry, and they live inside-the-beltline Raleigh. David's daughter attends Enloe High School and is active in musical theater. When they are not working, you are most likely to find them rooting for the Carolina Hurricanes or Alabama Crimson Tide football, enjoying a live performance at DPAC or Memorial Hall at UNC, or trying out one of the Triangle's hottest new restaurants.

Buying or Selling a Home in the Indianapolis Area

Mike Deck

Introduction

"Since 1992, repeat customers, loyal clients and friends, who trust us to create win-win situations by following the Golden Rule, are the reason for our company's success," said Mike Deck, Broker/Owner of ERA Real Estate Links and leader of **Team Deck** in Carmel, Indiana.

For Mike and his team, this strategy proves to be very attractive to clients and agents alike. While Team Deck is comprised of seven members, ERA Real Estate Links has over 30 agents, is ranked in the top 1% of more than 3,000 ERA offices nationwide, and is one of the leading real estate companies in greater Indianapolis. Since the year 2010, Team Deck has been the #1 agent in Carmel and Westfield in Total Production. Team Deck is the #1 Broker Team for ERA and consistently ranks in the top 5 of all MIBOR agents. Team Deck's Career Volume exceeds

$750,000,000 and with over 75 Years combined experience in the business, Team Deck brings a wealth of knowledge and wisdom to their clients.

Mike grew up in Carmel and graduated from Carmel High School. He has an extensive network within the community and industry. After graduating from Hanover College, he worked in the corporate world for a while, but his desire to remain in his community and his growing love of construction brought him to real estate. His trustworthy personality, his Golden Rule philosophy, and his value for strong relationship building have certainly contributed to the success of ERA Real Estate Links.

Mike Deck entered the Real Estate industry in 1992 and has been serving buyers and sellers in the Northern suburbs of Indianapolis since that time. Mike primarily works with the higher-end, custom home market in Carmel, Fishers, Westfield, and Zionsville, Indiana. From assisting clients with the purchase of their dream home to helping families relocate to the area, Mike is the expert!

In this chapter, Mike Deck provides insights for potential buyers and sellers in the Indianapolis area.

Selling Your Indianapolis Area Home

Most who are thinking about selling their home in Indianapolis are planning to stay and purchase in the area. Fortunately, the Indianapolis area has gone through tremendous growth and continues to grow, especially in new construction. When clients contact us, they most often are interested in the assistance of selling their home as well as the purchase of a new home. The first step is to have a conversation with the client(s) about their goals and objectives for making a move. What are they looking for in a new home? What are the financial objectives and budget? What are their needs - the most important characteristics of a new home? What are their desires? Putting these in priority order will help ensure that the client(s) and agent are on the same page.

The activity in our real estate market is heavily based around the school schedule. Families with children that will be attending a different school after the move generally put their home on the market in March. This allows the client(s) time to find a home and move in before the start of the new school year.

Understanding the market value and how to price a home accordingly is a major factor in selling a home in a reasonable amount of time. We do a market analysis on the home, comparing it to similar homes that have recently sold in the neighborhood or wider area, but more importantly we look at the competition and rank the home against others to ensure the home is priced as competitively as possible. Once we determine the estimated market value, we have a discussion with the seller on the actual pricing strategy for the listing. When establishing a list price, it's important to understand how buyers are searching for homes.

Most homebuyers are searching online and usually searching in a specific price range for what they are expecting to pay. We tailor the list price to maximize the opportunity for the home to be found in appropriate price bands. Let's say we have determined the fair market price is $685,000. How do we attract the most buyers for a home around this price? Prospective buyers for this home might be searching in several price ranges: $600,000 to $700,000; $650,000 to $750,000; or $700,000 to $800,000. In this case we might suggest pricing at $700,000. At this price, the home will show up in all of the likely price ranges that the buyers will be searching. If we were to price at $699,000, we would miss the buyers looking at $700,000+.

One misconception we occasionally encounter is the idea that the home should be priced at a large margin above the real market value. Some would think that this leaves room for negotiations and therefore a reduction in price if it does not sell. Let's say our seller wanted to price the same home for $750,000, expecting to ultimately sell for a lower amount. Now, what happens is the buyers searching around the true market value of $650,000 to $700,000 will not even see the home when they search online. New listings generate the most activity and the highest and best offers usually come in the first 30 days of listing the home. Overpricing dramatically reduces the traffic, and helps sell other competitively priced homes instead of your home. This strategy leads to one or more price reductions causing potential buyers to question what could potentially be wrong with the home. Buyers always want to know "why hasn't this house sold yet," so telling them the house was overpriced doesn't always ease their mind; they are convinced it is something else.

When we put your home on the market, our number one marketing strategy is setting the best first impression. Whether it's viewing online photos or an in-person showing, we only have a few seconds to attract attention and make that crucial first impression. We won't put a home on the market until it is ready. How long will it take? Each situation is different, and we will guide you through what should be done. I can assure them that we will have it on the market within 24 hours after all of our photography is completed, but not before we have perfect photography!

The first thing to look at is the exterior, especially the front yard and front of the house. The landscaping should be trimmed, mulched, and fertilized to bring out as much green in the lawn as possible. Fresh flowers will add some nice color. Being a fairly seasonal climate in Indiana, our homes in April to November are going to show better than in the winter period from December to March. If someone is going to list in the spring and we know in advance, we will take the pictures the prior fall as it takes a while for things to turn in Indiana. The front door needs to be painted or stained and new door hardware added. Any cobwebs should be removed and any outside light fixtures that are rusted or broken should be replaced. Chipped paint should at least be touched up as well. The home needs to appear that it has been well maintained all the time.

Inside the home we want to adapt as much as possible to the current trends in colors and décor without the client having to spend too much money. The majority is done through paint and de-cluttering, which are the lowest cost methods of transforming a home. Depending on the age, style, and condition of some features, we may recommend additional changes to floors, countertops, or fixtures. It's a multi-step process in helping the client determine how to achieve the best result while spending as little as possible. For some houses, that might be $500, and for others it might be $15,000. Of course, it depends on the client's objectives and willingness to invest with a good short-term return on the investment. The bottom line is putting a home on the market without preparing it for sale is disastrous.

Once painting or any physical changes are completed, we'll have our team assist in de-cluttering and rearranging of furniture. We want to make sure all of the rooms look great when we do the photo shoot. There is a wide variety of quality photography in online real estate listings, but there is no substitute for professional photography when we are making that first impression online. Our marketing for luxury properties also incorporates 3D virtual tours, videos, and drone photography. All of which go beyond the luxury of the property by showcasing the style, location, proximity to amenities, and lifestyle of the home.

Our objective when marketing the home is to price and present it in a manner for it to sell within 30 days. With the vast majority of buyers starting their search for a home online, it's important to get the home in showcase positions on the major real estate websites to maximize the number of potential buyers that see the listing. We invest quite a bit of money to make sure our listings are elevated in position in buyers' searches. Interestingly, our listings attract buyer attention to the extent that about 35% of our listings are sold through direct buyer contact.

In today's world people expect immediate access to information. In response, our For-Sale signs have a number to text for further information on the home. When an interested buyer is in front of the home and they text the number on the sign, information on that house will show up on their phone and then our other listings in the area also show up. This allows an interested buyer to receive immediate information on the home as well as information on other homes we have listed in the area. The text alerts an agent on our team whom can then communicate with the potential buyer and set up a potential showing.

As soon as a home is listed, the client should be prepared for showings. Showings can be scheduled a day or two in advance and sometimes with very little notice. Therefore, it is important to keep the home clean and tidy during this period. We recommend to any seller(s) with pets that they take them out of the home during showings or have them kept in kennels, as their presence unfortunately tends to be a leading issue with showings.

The proper presentation of a home can lead to one or more offers. In order to help our client(s) negotiate offers, we not only need to understand what is important to our client, but also what is important to the buyer. It is not always the price; possession and other factors frequently come into play as well.

Successful negotiations result in a win-win transaction in which both the buyer and seller are happy after the deal is completed. Ninety-nine percent of our deals end up at the closing table because we truly work to make it a win-win transaction for both parties. It's critical to help find a middle ground that works for everyone involved.

As mentioned earlier, with about 35% of our listings, the buyer contacts us to represent them on the buying side, which is well above the typical statistic in our market. With our team's Golden Rule philosophy of making every transaction a win-win for both parties, we can faithfully represent both the buyer and seller in the same transaction. In this regard, we are very upfront with both parties. Communication is key, and as a mediator it is important that I put together a deal that works for both parties. I serve as a middleman making sure both parties understand what's important to the other, while not disclosing any information that would hurt either party. When both parties truly understand what's important to the other, it helps them get to an agreeable solution that works for everybody and in a shorter period of time.

Buying Your Indianapolis Area Home

On the buying side, the first step should be to get a good understanding of your particular financial situation, including the price of a home that you can afford, as well as a monthly budget that makes you comfortable. Unless you are paying all cash, mortgage financing will be needed, so you will need to get a good idea of the amount of loan that you can qualify for. It doesn't make sense to start looking for a home until you know the price of home you can afford. We want to make sure our buyers are pre-qualified before looking at homes. Another point is that without a pre-qualification letter, sellers and their agents may not consider your offer, especially in an active market. This advice applies to all income levels and even relatively wealthy individuals or families can have some difficulty getting qualified, because they may have a complex financial situation, owning multiple properties or businesses. You should also make sure that a home purchase works in your long-term financial plan. We recommend that you meet with one of our preferred lenders that have a good track record of accurately pre-qualifying buyers and that can get the loans closed in a timely manner.

It is important to communicate with your agent the must haves and wants in order to better understand what you are looking for. This is generally done in an introductory meeting we have with a client. Sometimes an interactive discussion helps crystalize the real priorities. Are you looking for a larger garage or yard? Do you have children and are looking to move based on the school? What nearby amenities are important to you? It is important to prioritize because you're usually not going to get everything you want unless you custom build from scratch on the lot of your dreams. Setting this expectation up front keeps clients from getting discouraged with the home find process.

Most clients moving within the local area have a relatively good idea of the specific areas that are of interest. Therefore, it is a matter of finding the ideal home within their budget. We also work with a number of clients moving from other states that are usually not as familiar with the area. We have our own internal relocation division called Relocation Links that performs the duties of a relocation company. We've become their one-stop shop to find out everything there is to know about Indianapolis. Most people visiting for the first time are surprised to observe the sophistication of our school systems, the ease of getting around with fantastic traffic flow, the cleanliness of the city, and all the amenities we have to offer. Our geographic focus is centered on Carmel and the surrounding suburbs, north of downtown Indianapolis. The area to the north of Indianapolis has some of the best public schools, and is generally the location of choice for executives and their families relocating into the area. *Money Magazine's* 2017 annual ranking of *The Best Places to Live in America* ranked one of our suburbs at Number 1 and two others in the top 25.

As we work with buyers to identify the best properties for them, we provide a market analysis on the area and specific homes that they are interested in. This assures that they understand the fair market value and are not paying too much. People coming from other areas should be aware that Indiana has a very stable home market without large shifts in either direction. It is important to buy something that will work for you for several years, allowing good equity to build over time.

In structuring an offer, price is always a major point, but we also want to learn what else is important to the seller. As I mentioned before, our objective is to make the transaction a win-win for both parties. With a good understanding of what is important to both sides we can structure an offer that is more likely to result in a completed transaction that is satisfactory to all.

After we have negotiated the purchase contract, there are several steps to complete before the purchase is finalized and closed. We provide a very detailed letter with all the timelines required to complete inspections and remove contingencies. It is critical to stay on track with these steps or buyers can risk losing their earnest money deposit. Inspections result in a report that may be a bit difficult to interpret, so we have a contracting team that will assess everything in the inspection report. Some findings may indicate that we should ask the seller to correct certain problems and that may lead to further negotiations to put together a fair solution for both parties. You can't expect everything to be perfect on a resale house, so some findings may just be maintenance items that will be the responsibility of the buyer.

Buying a home can be a complex journey that can be much easier with less stress when working with an experienced agent that has an abundance of local knowledge.

What Clients Are Saying

"We have moved 17 times and Team Deck has provided the best overall service that we have ever received. Their ability to provide a smooth and stress-free approach during our recent home transition is truly unique. They have now duplicated that level of service on multiple buy/sell transactions for us. I now look to them for referral assistance when selecting my other residential services. A trusted partner for us."

—Kevin & Jackie R.

"Team Deck sold two homes for us over the past 9 months...a home and a townhouse. We were very impressed with their expertise and knowledge of the two different markets required to sell our properties. For both homes, their negotiating skills enabled us to get close to our asking price. When we listed our townhouse we had already relocated to AZ so we were totally dependent on Team Deck for everything. They did an incredible job including working with our tenants and making sure everything went smoothly for the closing. Their marketing strategy is amazing, and their response to e-mails, phone calls or texts is always timely. They make it very easy to do business with them because everything is handled "in house". So...take the stress and hassle of selling your house: CHOOSE TEAM DECK!"

—Carl & Jane S.

"Mike is a great agent and I would highly recommend using him. I have worked with him twice and both times he did a great job. I would use him again. Mike told me exactly what I needed to do to sell my house and it sold in two days for exactly the price I wanted."

—Scott & Karen P.

"The most professional and personable Real Estate agent we've ever been associated with. Mike has sold two homes for us and assisted in the purchase of another one. I highly recommend Mike Deck!"

—Dennis & Lori C.

"Mike helped our family relocate to a neighborhood closer to our daughter's school. Selling a home is stressful, but he helped guide us through the process in a calming manner. In addition, he was very helpful with finding us quality contractors when minor repairs were needed before closing. He is very knowledgeable about Carmel real estate and assisted us greatly in finding the right home. We would use Mike again for any future real estate transactions."

—Jeff & Tiffany C.

"Mike does a great job and has a great team that will make your buying and/or selling experience a much smoother transition than imaginable. They are second to none."

—Russ and Emily K.

Selecting an Agent

Your home is one of your most valuable financial assets. When you are planning to buy and/or sell a home, selecting the right real estate agent to help you throughout the process can make a big difference in your outcome as well as your peace of mind. Anyone can get an abundance of information online today, but what is missing is the insight to help you make the right decisions regarding the purchase or sale of a home.

Extensive detailed knowledge of the area is the most important factor in selecting an agent. It's the things you can't find online where an experienced agent can be most valuable. Knowledge of homes coming to the market before they hit the market can also be valuable, especially in the recent period where we have limited inventory. Background information on the city or town, the council members, and future plans may all have a bearing on making a good decision.

Reviewing testimonials can provide some information on how past clients have viewed their experience with an agent. I would suggest choosing one that has a reputation for working really hard on the behalf of their clients. Real estate is a personal relationship business. You'll be working closely with your agent during a concentrated period so choosing one that is compatible from a personality standpoint is usually important. Finally, with a lot of money at stake in any real estate transaction, it is important that you can trust that your agent is always looking out for your best interests during the process.

About Mike Deck

Mike Deck is the Broker/Owner of ERA Real Estate Links in Carmel, Indiana, with over 30 real estate agents. He is also the leader of Team Deck, comprised of seven members. Team Deck is the #1 ERA Broker team in the country and consistently ranks in the top 5 of all agents in the Indianapolis area.

Mike grew up in Carmel, Indiana and after graduating from Hanover College, he worked briefly in the corporate world. He had a desire to stay in the community and his interest in construction led him to the real estate industry in 1992. He has been helping buyers and sellers with their real estate transaction in Carmel and the surrounding northern suburbs of Indianapolis since that time.

Mike is involved in several community organizations in Carmel and surrounding towns. He supports Grace Church, The Matthew 25 Center at Our Lady of Mt. Carmel, Fellowship of Christian Athletes, Riley Children's Hospital, and Open Doors in Westfield. He also served on the original board that helped create Westfield's Grand Park, the largest family sports complex in the country.

For more information about Mike Deck, visit www.RealEstateLinks.com/find-an-agent/MikeDeck.

Maximize Profit When Selling Your Home

Matt Bauscher

Introduction

After a successful career in basketball, both at the collegiate and professional level, Matt Bauscher earned a Masters degree and decided to get involved in real estate. Being a strong competitor on the court and in life he wanted to work in a competitive field where there is no ceiling.

Matt is the founding partner of Amherst Madison Real Estate Advisors, a real estate agency in Boise, Idaho. He excels in aiding buyers and sellers with their residential real estate transactions in the greater Boise area. Matt is noted for his expertise in the luxury home market, and he is responsible for a high percentage of the luxury home sales in the area, among over 7,000 agents.

Matt became the youngest real estate agent in Idaho history to sell over 100 properties in 3 consecutive years—2016, 2017, and 2018—and was voted the Number 1 real estate agent in the Boise area. In 2017 and 2018 alone he personally surpassed well over $100 million in sales.

In this chapter Matt Bauscher provides great insights for residential property sellers.

Selling Your Home

I've often observed that homeowners wait until they are ready to sell before contacting an agent for the first time. There's a lot of information out there on TV and the Internet about home improvements and fixing up your home. Without the context of the current local market situation and realistically estimating return on investment, many homeowners start spending money without the insight of what really is going to maximize the net profit. There are usually some obvious repairs that are needed, but many replacements and improvements will not return an investment dollar-for-dollar. Even if it's six months or a year before you want to sell, I recommend making contact with an experienced agent who can provide appropriate advice on getting the home ready as soon as you are considering selling. The more time we have, the better the preparation, as well as the results.

When initially talking with your agent, it's important to be as clear as possible in communicating your objectives for a sale. The more information we have, the better we can serve you. What is the reason you are selling? What is the timeframe? What made you purchase the home? Are there any problems that you foresee? What are your expectations from an agent? By fully understanding your situation, we can customize a tailored approach and develop a plan to achieve your goals.

Pricing the home is typically one of the first considerations a seller has when they are contemplating a sale. The local market and a willing buyer determine the value, not the seller or the agent. It's critical to establish the best estimate of the value before setting the listing price. Tens of thousands of dollars are won and lost every day because of agents. Square footage is always one factor to consider but is often the most over-rated statistic in selling a home. This is similar to asking my wife how much her shoes cost per pound. Lot size, views, garage size, layout, upgrades – none of these have anything to do with price per square foot.

In our Competitive Market Analysis (CMA) we review the details on a number of most comparable recent sales, making adjustments for relevant differences, such as location, size, amenities, level of finishes, age. This shows a "rear view mirror" summary of actual recent sales. We also look at pending sales which shows us the current market snapshot. There is an art to coming up with a precise pricing range on the estimated value and very seldom is there a disagreement after we go through and explain our analysis. I provide an informed analysis on value based on motivation and market condition.

One challenge with the CMA is that it is based on sales generally one to six months in arrears. It's also critical to look at the current competition as well as the current market conditions. Even more than the sold comps, the competition tells an important story. What's the best available home in the area in a relevant price range? What are the average amount of days on market and the level of inventory? There are a lot of misconceptions about pricing strategy. For example, many people think that you should start out high and negotiate or drop the price if you don't get your price. Unfortunately, this strategy is most likely to get you a lower price in the end. We have to sell your home to three different groups: buyers, buyer's agents, and the appraiser. They are comparing your home to the competing homes on the market and are not likely to be fooled by an unreasonably high price. The result is the listing becomes stale and it languishes on the market. Then you have to reduce the list price and buyers wonder what is wrong with the house. In addition, an overpriced listing will help sell your competitors' homes. Buyers often view 5 different homes and then make an offer on the best priced property that fits their needs.

Many times in a seller's market where homes in your neighborhood are receiving multiple offers to the extent there is a bidding war, we consider pricing at the lower end of the range and let the buyers bid against each other driving the price to the higher end or above our estimated value range. Pricing with great value for a buyer will draw immediate showings and activity. Every situation needs to be carefully considered and insight from an experienced agent can guide you to a strategy that maximizes your profit upon sale. Making a mistake with the listing price can cost a seller thousands.

Listing your home during the busiest time of the market is not always the best option. There is less inventory and also fewer buyers in the first quarter, but there are many buyers that need to purchase at different times of the year. In the less active times the potential buyers are generally real buyers, so depending on your situation it can still be a good time to list as the showings may be less in quantity but higher in quality. We also need to consider your neighborhood situation. As an example, near the end of the year we look at your neighborhood and there's not a single home on the market in your subdivision, but we know there are going to be six coming on the market in the Spring. It might be a great time to list before competition hits the market.

One of the most important aspects of getting the highest price and return on investment is getting the home correctly prepared for sale. First impressions and curb appeal are crucial. Look at the landscaping and make sure it is in proper shape – no weeds, beds nicely covered with mulch, lawn kept cut. Any kind of deferred maintenance needs to be taken care of. Look around both the exterior and interior for signs of peeled paint, dings, torn or stained carpet, holes in drywall, broken windows, or other minor cosmetic issues that are likely to be noticed. Potential buyers are going to notice these problems and that gets them wondering what other problems exist that they can't see. Many of these small issues don't have to cost that much and some you may be able to handle yourself. Of course, major maintenance issues, where equipment is not functioning or where there is major damage, need to be addressed or there will be significant difficulty in attracting buyers. The objective is to be able to present a clean, well-maintained home to potential buyers.

Buyers tend to discount the value by much more than the cost of repairs. They imagine the cost to fix is a lot higher than actual. Let's say they imagine it will cost them $10,000 to take care of fixing problems. They may not have the additional $10,000 to handle the repairs. Instead they likely would rather pay $10,000 more for the home, including that amount in the mortgage. The same $10,000 included in their loan, will only cost about $50 more per month with a 30-year fixed rate loan.

Another frequent mistake is making changes before selling without understand potential return on investment. Let's say you have plastic laminate kitchen counters (Formica®) or similar product). Quartz and Granite counters are in style, and it's easy to think updating the counters will make a positive impact on the transaction profit. You remove the laminate counters and may have lost $1,000 of value. Now you replace with granite counters that cost $4,000. At best you have a net value increase of $3,000, only 75% return on investment. If the laminate counters are clean, not cracked or stained, you're probably better off keeping the counters. Some buyers may like the granite, but they may not like the color you choose while others might actually prefer laminate or an alternate counter surface. As mentioned earlier, it's better to consult with an experienced agent prior to making changes or installing high-end finishes to make sure you're maximizing net profit.

After addressing items that need to be repaired or cleaned, the home needs to be as light, bright, and open as possible. The less furniture and the less clutter you have in the house, the bigger it's going to feel. We want potential buyers to imagine themselves living in it. We have a staging consultant we bring in to offer detail suggestions on furnishing arrangement. We can remove furniture, change locations within certain rooms, or completely stage the home. It's a tailored approach for each individual seller.

All the family photos need to be taken down. When buyers are walking through the home their eyes will be drawn to faces and all of a sudden, they aren't looking at the house. It's difficult for people visiting the house to look at portraits of a couple in the master bedroom and imagine themselves living there. Everyone has different views on a number of topics so you should remove anything of a religious or political nature. It's easy to alienate people. I've had buyers not purchase a particular house because of a political saying or a poster on the wall. You will need to pack up when you move anyway, so it's better to pack up and store personal items and extra furniture in a storage unit or pod.

Studies have shown that about 95% of buyers looking for a home start their search on the Internet. Your first impression online is vital as you only have seconds to attract attention. Typically, buyers won't even read the narrative or about the amenities if the photos don't interest them. We have the best professional photographer do the photo shoot for every one of my listings, whether it's a $1 million listing or a $300,000 listing. Consistent marketing is vital.

In order to obtain top dollar when we are marketing the home, we're not just trying to sell a house, but the lifestyle as well – the amenities, the local parks, schools, hiking trails, access to the river, foothills. We use a lot of lifestyle photos that are incorporated along with the house photos so viewers can appreciate the lifestyle as well as the home.

Drone photography can help if the home has a view, is situated adjacent to open land, or is in proximity to significant amenities. From eye level it's hard to see the surroundings in a picture. On higher-end listings we incorporate different marketing packages to showcase the property.

I believe it's important to start building excitement as the property is going on the market. As we are getting ready for the listing to go live we start exposing it privately to other local agents, letting them know the listing is coming. We also have thousands of people in our database and we match up potential buyers and let them know about the upcoming listing.

I believe in using top notch marketing materials that won't get thrown away because the quality is too nice. These are created before the listing is active, so we are all ready with everything in advance. Whether someone walks through the home and wants the house or not, the flyer is nice enough they're going to take it and leave it on their coffee table for friends and family to see. We also do an outreach to neighbors. We generally like to let the immediate neighbors know of the listing and suggest that it gives them an opportunity to pick their neighbor by letting their friends know about the home.

As soon as the property officially goes on the market, we're actively marketing the listing through the multiple listing service (MLS), as well as hundreds of websites. We also promote on social media. As the time changes, so does the marketing approach. What worked 10 years ago often needs to be reevaluated as technology and end user habits change.

We observe listings going live just about any time during the week, but I incorporate a strategy that gives the most initial impact. Buyers focus their attention on new listings and we want our new listing to show up when buyers are more likely to be looking. Early in the week is not the best time. On Monday, most people are putting their head down; they're catching up and in work mode. They're not in house hunting mode or relax mode. Then as the week goes on, they start looking towards the weekend. By Thursday people are psychologically in a better mood than Monday. They're less busy and not as stressed. They may be interested in looking at homes over the weekend and are ready to look online to line up homes to see. We always try to post our listings early Thursday morning and we schedule an open house on that weekend. In an active market we are getting lots of qualified buyers through the home by Saturday or Sunday.

Once the home listing goes active, keeping your home in clean and in show-ready condition and providing access for buyer showings is critical. Access is one of the most underappreciated aspects of selling a home, but with coordination among the agents, buyers, and the seller necessary to gain access for showings, it can limit the ability to get people through the home and thus hinders the ability to get top dollar. Since we try to create a lot of buzz around the first full weekend after the listing, I recommend that the sellers be away from the home for a few days – either on vacation or with friends or relatives. We try to make the first few days a very active time, maximizing showings, and hopefully generating multiple offers.

The optimal situation is for the seller to completely move out of the home in advance if they can financially afford it. This may involve moving in with extended family, finding a short-term rental, or getting a bridge loan to purchase a new property in advance. Sometimes it takes a creative solution. In a recent case our seller was planning to pay cash for a new home after the current home sold. In this case the seller was able to purchase a new home with a five-year ARM loan at a low rate. The seller moved to the new home and when the sale of the former home closed, was able to pay off the temporary loan with cash proceeds from the sale.

With the initial buzz that we create, offers might start coming in rapidly after going on the market, particularly in an active marketplace. I caution against accepting any offer within the first 24 hours of going on the market, because there has not been time to get enough buyers through the home.

Negotiating strategy depends on market conditions. In a seller's market, leverage is on the side of the seller, but the price is not the only important term. There may be multiple offers, but we want to have a high confidence level that the buyer with the offer we negotiate will be able to close. Inspection contingency period is one example. How many days should be allowed? An aggressive approach is to allow a 3 to 5-day inspection contingency with earnest money non-refundable after. Is the buyer willing to bring more cash into the deal if the appraisal does not come in at the agreed-upon price? Of course, we don't even consider offers unless financing is approved in advance or they supply proof of funds in an all-cash purchase. Contingencies on sale of the buyer's own property is an obstacle unless their home is already under contract and they are willing to put skin in the game with non-refundable earnest money or a bump clause that gives the seller the right to continue to market it.

Selecting the Best Agent for You

A common misconception is that all agents are alike, and it doesn't matter who you engage to sell your home. Is it possible that the person that sells only 5 homes per year provides the same results as another that sells 125 per year? Tens of thousands of dollars are won or lost every day in the intelligent preparation of properties as well in the negotiations of the contract.

The first thing to check is the experience level, including how many homes the agent is selling every year. What is the amount of volume, average price point, average days on the market? Ask for references and check with them what their experiences were like. Look at past marketing efforts. Does the agent have the resources to spend on marketing and provide vast market exposure for your home? When reviewing marketing campaigns, can you see the difference in marketing that makes the home stand out among others on the market? How well connected is the agent?

Another point to check is the level of support behind the agent. Does the agent do everything by themselves or is there a support staff reinforcing the agent? Once the deal goes pending, who ensures that everything will be taken care of in a timely manner? My team is available seven days a week to address any matters that arise. Homes sell seven days a week.

What Clients Are Saying

"Matt gets the job done and is a pleasure to work with. He is an excellent negotiator and always has his client's best interests at heart.

He will go above and beyond to make sure that your rather large investment is the right one for you."

—Lorie T.

"We had tried the year previously to sell our home but we only had a couple of showings for the whole 2 month period it was listed with another realtor. Then we met Matt Bauscher from a referral from our neighbors. From the moment we met him we knew he was a guy that would be able to sell our home. He was very confident and that made us confident that we would finally be able to sell. He advertised it to everyone and we got tons of showings! It took about the timeframe he said it would and we got an offer! Amazingly he got us our Christmas miracle and we were able to simultaneously close on the property we were selling and get into a wonderful new property at the same time! Not going to say it was an easy process but in the end he got us EXACTLY what we wanted. We are so grateful that we met him because he and his crew, Alicia and Kory, were amazing from the beginning to the end! We highly recommend working with the Matt Bauscher team."

—Maureena & Matt

"Matt was phenomenal in helping us not only sell our home with a full price offer in just a few days, but purchasing and closing on a new home in less than a month. We have been more than impressed with his knowledge of the market and how seamless he has made the process multiple times. No question Bauscher Real Estate is the best in Idaho!!!"

—Taylor S.

"Matt and his team was absolutely a pleasure to deal with. They were very responsive and took care of all the small details in a very timely manner. I would highly recommend them!!"

—Donald F.

"Matt sold our house in December and we were very pleased with his work! We interviewed many realtors before deciding to use Matt. We chose him because there was no doubt that he would do whatever it took to get our house sold, and that's exactly what he did. He created exceptionally high quality marketing materials including a fantastic video that showcased our house in a superb manor. We almost didn't want to move after seeing the video! We had a few stumbling blocks along the way, as with any sale, but Matt worked diligently to ensure they were all resolved. Despite our discerning requirements for a new home and looking at about every house in Boise, Eagle and Meridian, Matt and Kory worked patiently and tirelessly to finally find us our new home. Kory exemplified Matt's high standards as he objectively showed us house after house…we really appreciated his work. By this glowing review you might think we are related (ha-ha), but we had never met Matt before this sale. He will definitely be our realtor for our next sale."

—Holly & Ralph K.

"I called Matt, with the hope of getting a plan set to sell our house in a year, after we made all the necessary repairs. On our first meeting Matt took the time to listen to what my husband and I wanted to do. After that meeting we went from a game plan of selling and buying in a year to putting our home on the market in the weeks that

followed. Matt and his team worked hard to get our home listed in a timely manner but that also looked its best. Once we were on the market, our first offer came through in 4 days, we were shocked on how fast it happened, but the offer fell through. And what impressed me the most about Matt was his confidence in selling our home and not letting that offer that had fallen through affect our mentality. His confidence was very genuine, we knew he wasn't worried and he had the highest amount of confidence in his team, so we didn't worry. We then moved to buying our next dream home. Matt and his team did an amazing job at keeping us grounded showing us options that really worked for us and our budget. They worked so hard to find us the right home. We were so happy to have worked with the lending company Matt sent us over to and the title company we closed with. Matt has relationships with the best people in the industry and he gave us the best. We cannot say it enough, but we are so thankful we connected with Matt. He helped us accomplish another goal and we so grateful for that!"

—Benny & Hortensia H.

About Matt Bauscher

Matt Bauscher is the owner of Bauscher Real Estate and the founding partner of Amherst Madison Real Estate Advisors in Boise, Idaho. He represents buyers and sellers in their residential real estate transactions. He graduated with a Bachelors degree from Boise State University and a Masters Degree from Concordia University. While at Boise State, Matt played on the basketball team where he earned a number of awards and won the conference championship. After college he played professional basketball in Europe where he won multiple MVP awards and a national championship.

Matt's competitive spirit has quickly led to success in real estate and provides a great client experience. Matt is noted for his expertise in the Boise area luxury home market. He has consistently sold over 100 homes in consecutive years (in 2016, 2017, and 2018). Matt was voted the Number 1 real estate agent in the Boise area and was responsible for over $100 million in real estate sales in just his last two years.

For more information about Matt Bauscher, visit http://www.BauscherRealEstate.com.

Buying and Selling Homes in the Chattanooga Area

Cheryl and Brad Fuqua

Introduction

After a career in the medical industry, Cheryl Fuqua pursued a completely different path and became a licensed real estate agent in 2000. She primarily helps sellers in the Chattanooga region with their real estate transactions and has been a consistent award winner for listings and sales production. Cheryl is a Certified Residential Specialist (CRS), the highest designation for real estate agents who work with residential clients. She is also an Accredited Buyers Representative (ABR).

Cheryl's son, Brad Fuqua, joined her real estate practice in 2013, and he specializes in helping buyers find their ideal home in the Chattanooga area. He works with first time homebuyers, investors, and people relocating to the Chattanooga region.

Cheryl and Brad are affiliated with the Hixson, Tennessee office of Keller Williams, where Brad is the managing broker.

In this chapter, they provide insights for buyers and sellers. Although based on their nearly 25 years of combined experience in buying and selling in Chattanooga, these key principles are the foundation for a successful home sale or purchase—no matter where you call home.

Home Sale Strategies That Work

The decision to sell a home is often dependent on many factors. Whatever your reason for selling, our proven effective market strategies combined with professional, ethical and confidential service have helped our clients get the highest possible price for their home. Pricing is often the initial consideration for homeowners—and for good reason. Everyone has an emotional attachment to their home and likely have an idea about the price they would like to receive. The reality is that the market sets the price and you will be best served with an objective evaluation of market value based on solid information and facts. We start with a review of the most comparable recent home sales in your neighborhood and nearby areas. Elements of value include location, condition and presentation, level of finishes and upgrades, size of home and lot, the view, level of home sales activity in the neighborhood, and amenities. We compare the differences among the most similar properties to your home and adjust for the differences in coming up with an estimate of market value. As this is being written we have experienced a tight market with a low level of inventory, so sometimes we need to go out as much as five miles to get enough comparable sales data. We need to think in terms of how an appraiser will view your home and use a similar analysis method.

Understanding what upgrades you have made to your home is important when comparing sales data to estimate a value. We had a recent example where just the past sales data alone didn't tell the entire story. Less than a year after the homeowners purchased their home, the husband was transferred, so now they need to sell. They had expected to stay in the area long-term, so they did a beautiful upgrade to their kitchen. Our analysis shows the improvement added $20,000 more to the value compared to when they purchased the home. Agents and buyers can see the past sales data and will likely notice that the price is considerably higher than the selling price just a year earlier. To rationalize the difference we have pictures of the home as it appeared when purchased, as well as current pictures, so interested buyers can understand the reason for the value increase.

The highest level of buyer activity—and the best opportunity for the seller—is right after we put the home on the market. With knowledge of the market value, it's critical to be properly positioned against the competition at the time of listing. A home that is priced appropriately to the market and is also presented well is more likely to attract buyers and multiple offers in a short period of time.

Testing the market by overpricing at a considerable amount over market value is never a good idea. You won't get the buyer traffic and are much less likely to attract any offers at all. What generally happens in this situation is the home sits on the market, you have to drop the price anyway, and potential buyers wonder what is wrong with the home. This strategy most often results in a lower sales price and a much longer time on the market.

Underpricing a home is another strategy sometimes deployed in a strong market. Hoping for multiple offers and a bidding war to drive up the price is a risky strategy— and there is no guarantee you will get multiple offers.

Along with a good pricing strategy, how your home looks is critical to making the sale. We need to look a the home "through the buyer's eyes." Curb appeal is the first thing to review. As a potential buyer is parking and walking up to your front door, what do they see? That first impression will give them a sense of what they are expecting to see inside. A manicured and well-kept yard, mulch in the flowerbeds, and a cut lawn all provide good indicators of how well the home has been maintained. Is the mailbox in good condition? Is the front door freshly painted or stained? Are there flowers planted to provide some color? Does the doorbell ring? Are the windows clean?

Inside the home, everything that needs repair should be addressed. Dings in the walls or the baseboards should be fixed. Walls with scratches or worn paint should be repainted. Small points shouldn't be overlooked. Are there working light bulbs in all of the light fixtures? Homes with lots of natural light are more inviting, so removal of some window treatment may be advised.

Of course, the big items like the roof and heating and air conditioning systems should be in good condition. If there are any issues, they need to be corrected. Keep in mind that after a contract is signed the buyer will have an inspection conducted. Old heating and air equipment, near end of life, might be an issue when it comes to the inspection. Sometimes sellers have the money to replace old equipment and sometimes they don't, but it's better to be aware of problems that may arise in advance to minimize any surprises later.

When your house goes on the market, the objective is to present a bright, open, clean, and well-maintained home to potential buyers. Over the years, most people collect lots of personal items and may have their home filled with furniture and walls covered with pictures. This can detract from buyers fully appreciating your home. If the home is filled with furniture, buyers will have a hard time imagining how their furniture will fit and the home will appear smaller. Too many pictures or artwork on the walls will attract attention away from the home itself. Even something like a curio cabinet that is completely filled gives the impression that everything is crowded and visitors may get focused on what is in the cabinet, not the house itself.

When you move you will need to pack up everything, so it's much better to do some decluttering before we put your home on the market. We'll walk through the home with you and provide a list of things that should be removed. Depending on the situation we will bring in a stager to consult on furniture arrangement that will open up the pathways as buyers are walking through the home and make it appear more spacious. Although we recommend depersonalizing while you are decluttering, it's important to keep one or two family pictures in the home, so people walking through can see who lives there.

After any cosmetic repairs have been completed, and your home has been decluttered and the furniture has been optimally arranged or staged, it's time to get high quality photos that will show off your home and its best features. Today, most potential buyers start their search for a home online and their first impression is from the initial photos they see there. We generally only have a few seconds to attract the attention of someone looking online, so professional photos that make a home stand out are critical. Virtual tours are another way we help the viewer get the feel of walking through the home. We also like to use drone photography when there is a view or adjacent land or amenities, so one can get a good sense of the surroundings. Depending on the property and its setting we may also include one or more twilight images. In addition to the online listings, photos are used in high quality flyers that are available to potential buyers visiting your home.

We create the biggest impact possible as soon as the home is listed by rapidly posting all of the photos, the description, and other information simultaneously as the Multiple Listing Service (MLS) listing goes live. When people rush to list and only put up one or two photos on the MLS, this leads to wondering what is wrong with the property. Our listings go on all of the major real estate websites, our personal website, and we also post on social media, playing up all the best features of the home.

Successfully marketing and selling your home is a lot more than getting it listed. Real estate is a relationship business and we work to maximize exposure among other real estate agents in the area. We send out the flyer to other agents within the Chattanooga area and make direct contact with agents specifically working in the area where the home is located to make sure they have information about the home and have seen it. With today's technology we are able to target buyers interested in a specific area or neighborhood, usually through Facebook.

When your home has been listed, it's critical to keep it clean, tidy, and ready to be shown with minimal notice. If you have pets, they should be removed, if possible. Pet bowls and blankets should be put away. Lights should be on and curtains kept open to get as much natural light as possible in. If no one is home during the day, the home should be left ready to show.

If the home is positioned and presented appropriately, it will attract one or more offers in a short period of time. You may have lived in the home a long time and had a lot of great experiences in the home, but it's important to remove emotions when you are selling. Consider the home a product at this point and think of the sale as a business transaction when reviewing offers. Some offers may not satisfy your requirements, but they can be a starting point. We believe that there is no bad offer. We'll help you evaluate the offers, as well as the buyers, and advise on counter-offer strategies. After an agreement is reached, we will navigate you through the buyer's inspections and any other contingency points that need to be resolved until your home is sold.

Your home is one of your most valuable financial assets, and a professional approach to selling it will help you generate the highest price in the shortest time.

What Sellers Are Saying

"Cheryl Fuqua is an excellent realtor and her kindness can be felt throughout the selling process. The effort put forth is hard to match when it comes to selling your home. In fact, my home sold in less than three days! Is that unusual - maybe, but her attention to details makes the process happen. If you are looking for a realtor with wisdom and grace - she is the perfect person."

—Kenneth M.

"Cheryl is a realtor who cares about the people she is working with. It is rare that you can't reach her, and if you have a question that she isn't sure about, you will quickly have an answer. Her team working in the background is wonderful as well. There is so much detail work that goes into the selling of your home, and the unseen team members keep the wheels turning. When the going gets tough, the tough keep going. That was our experience. The Fuqua Team Rocks!"

—Tammie Jo T.

"We hired Cheryl and Brad to help us sell our home and negotiate the buying of a new home. It was such a seamless process and they kept us stress free the entire time. They were so professional and easy to work with! I know we will never have to look for a new realtor again and will recommend them to everyone we know. Not to mention they got our house sold in 2 weeks! It doesn't get much better than that."

—Jessica R.

5 Steps to a Successful Home Buying Process

If you're thinking about buying a home for the first time, the process itself can feel daunting. The first part of our job is to educate our clients before guiding them through the stages of preapproval, creating a budget and a list of must-haves, and negotiating the sale. The next phase requires that we work together carefully through inspections—all the way to the closing table. By following these steps, we successfully help our clients find the right home at the right price.

1. Preapproval

The very first step when you are interested in buying a home is to contact a lender and get a preapproval letter. We've been in a very competitive market for buyers for a few years, and the buyer with preapproval will have a major advantage over buyers not already approved. You'll also get a precise understanding of the maximum home price you can qualify for, as well as what the monthly payments will be based on the loan amount. By talking with a lender, you will also get some insight on keeping your finances in order as you go through the home buying process. If you haven't already started working with a lender, we have recommended lenders that we know can help you get preapproved and that can close in a timely manner.

2. Budget & Must-Haves

After understanding your budget, make a list of what is important to you in a new home and put in priority order. What are the must-have characteristics? What are the like-to-haves? Watching real estate reality TV shows can give the impression that you can find everything you want in a home, but it's not always the actual case, even with new construction. By carefully clarifying your priorities and communicating them to your real estate agent, you will have a much better opportunity of realizing most, if not all, of your goals in a new home. We find that it's usually an interactive discussion, and as we ask clarifying questions our clients may change their minds on what is actually most important to them. Some typical considerations are location of work and how far they want to commute, preferred school zone, recreational interests, and nearby amenities.

3. Savvy Home Searching

Most homes for sale can now be found on the internet and some buyers wonder if they need an agent to help them find a home with all of the information available. The reality is that finding available homes is only a small part of the home buying process. Sure, you can just contact listing agents to see the homes you are interested in, but who is gong to represent you in the transaction? The listing agent on the sign or in the ad is looking out for the best interests of the seller – who is going to look out for your interests? Buyers are best served by using their own agent and it doesn't cost any more than working directly with the seller's agent, because the seller pays the full commission on both side of the transaction.

Focusing your home search online may result in missing properties that are not publicly listed, and additionally you may discount homes that are not well presented online. An experienced buyer's agent likely knows of properties you may not have been able to see online and may have knowledge of homes that fit your requirements that you may not have noticed. A buyer's agent will assist in analyzing and informing you of the fair market value as well as handling the negotiations to reach the best deal for you. After a contract is signed, we navigate our clients through the inspections, help resolve any issues that arise, and proceed to a closing.

Chattanooga and the surrounding area is attractive to a wide variety of people moving in from other states including quite a few people being relocated for work. For people new to the area, we take them on a tour of Chattanooga and the suburbs so they can get a feel of the many lifestyles and neighborhoods available. Our personal website has important and useful information about all of the different areas and townships around Chattanooga, including information about school ratings here in Hamilton County.

After understanding our client's objectives, preferences for neighborhoods, and budget, we organize a number of homes to visit that best match their criteria. These usually include some homes they have found online as well as others that we believe are a good fit. After a tour of homes, we'll go over the ones that are the top contenders and plan another detailed tour of those homes. Before making an offer on one of the homes, we will analyze the market value in a similar manner as if we were working with a seller. We'll look at comparable sales, typically over the past six months. It's a little more difficult in our current environment with limited inventory and a seller's market because many buyers are actually offering higher than what a market analysis shows on paper. The objective is for the buyer to have as much information as possible about the value to be able to make an informed offer.

4. Fair & Effective Offers

Some buyers think they should make a low ball offer to start negotiations. While this could work if the home is substantially overpriced with little buyer activity or during times where there are many more sellers than buyers, that is not generally recommended, especially in the type of market we have been experiencing in recent years. On the other hand, we don't recommend getting caught up in a buying frenzy and paying so much that you will regret it later. We recommend that a fair offer should be made, but unless the specific house is the one that you have to have no matter what, don't let other offers or the thought of losing the house influence your decision.

Before finalizing and presenting an offer, we work to gain insight from the seller's agent on the seller's motivations and objectives in the sale. With an understanding of the seller's needs, we can craft a compelling offer with terms other than just the price that will be most attractive. For example, the seller may want to be able to stay in the home until a new one is purchased. If our buyer has some flexibility in this area, we can accommodate the seller and make our offer stand out by adjusting the closing date out a bit longer than normal. Some buyers intend to pay in cash and have the ability to close rapidly if the seller prefers.

5. Home Inspection Help

After a purchase contract has been signed, the buyer has a contingency period to conduct inspections of the property. Buyers generally conduct a termite inspection and a general home inspection. The general inspection covers the roof, foundation, structure, and systems like the heating and air conditioning, plumbing and electrical. The inspections don't ensure that other problems will not be found after moving in, but they do provide peace of mind knowing the situation ahead of buying the home. We have a list of recommended inspectors that the buyer can use if they don't already have resources for the inspections. Keep in mind that the inspections need to be completed in a timely manner according to the terms of the contract and time should be reserved within that period for additional specialists to come in, if necessary.

If the inspections discover major issues that had not been previously disclosed, we help the buyer resolve the problems with the seller. Sometimes the resolution involves having the seller remedy the situation. In other cases, a price adjustment could be warranted, or the buyer may decline to purchase the property and get a refund of earnest money.

A home purchase is one of the most significant financial transactions individuals and families make in their life.

Working with an experienced agent can make the process of finding and purchasing the ideal home much smoother. When you work with us, we guide you through what can be a complicated process and provide information to enable you to purchase the right property at a fair price.

What Buyers Are Saying

"Brad did an outstanding job during our home buying process. He went above and beyond to make sure we were taken care of, was extremely prompt when replying to any questions or concerns we had and was willing to work with our busy schedules. When we would look at potential houses, he was always upfront if he noticed any issues with the house and never gave a salesman impression or tried to push us to make an offer. He was very patient and did a great job at making sure we were 100% satisfied with the terms of the negotiation process once we went under contract. We would recommend Brad to anyone looking to buy a home and would gladly work with him in the future."

—Amanda L.

"Brad's commitment to communication was fantastic. We had a lot of questions as first time home buyers. He was incredibly patient with us and explained many new and complicated situations easily. He made himself available for showings and questions whenever we needed it. His level of professionalism and experience were what we were hoping for in searching for our first home."

—Chris R.

"Brad was very attentive to our laundry list of wants/needs for our first home. He was constantly available by phone or text and even Face Timed us from potential homes when we were unable to make the trip to town. Brad was super knowledgeable about the town and quickly became a friend. I will absolutely recommend him to anyone!"

—Sarah T.

Selecting the Best Agent for You

Selling or purchasing a home can be an intense time, so selecting an agent that you feel you can trust and communicate with will be important to your ultimate satisfaction. When you are interviewing an agent, find out who you will be communicating with during different stages of the transaction and how communications will be handled. Follow up and rapid response times are critical in this business, so ask specifically about how they respond to questions and requests.

Look for someone with experience in the local market, with a large number of successful transactions. Experience over a number of economic cycles provides knowledge of how the real estate market reacts to varying conditions.

Education also demonstrates a focus on continuous improvement and excellence. A Certified Residential Specialist (CRS) is the highest industry designation for real estate agents who work with residential clients, and is a good indicator of an agent with good experience and a high level of transactions. A track record of success will give you a comfort level with the agent.

Financial advisors, insurance agents, and mortgage lenders are all good sources for referrals. Most successful agents have a good number of online reviews and testimonials that can be checked for reputation in handling real estate transactions.

As you are talking with an agent, consider their level of confidence in what they are saying. A confident professional will provide informed insight on the current market conditions and will be honest in their communications, even if it not what you want to hear. In the end, choose an agent that you believe will provide honest communications and one that you can trust will look out for your best interests.

About Cheryl and Brad Fuqua

Cheryl Fuqua became a licensed real estate agent in 2000, following a 20-year career in the medical industry. She has been a consistent award winner for listing and sales production, including the 2014 Top Team Award in the Chattanooga region. Cheryl is a Certified Residential Specialist (CRS), the highest designation for real estate agents who work with residential clients. She is also an Accredited Buyers Representative (ABR). Cheryl is an investor in Keller Williams and has served on the Agent Leadership Counsel, where she has encouraged professional development of new agents and fostered teamwork and ethical behavior in the workplace. She primarily helps sellers with their real estate transactions in the area.

With a great reputation in the real estate community, Cheryl has built her business by providing her customers insightful market knowledge and customer service that goes above and beyond expectations. She's a persistent negotiator and never gives up on helping her clients find the right home at the right price.

Brad Fuqua, Cheryl's son, joined her real estate practice and has been helping buyers find their ideal properties since 2013. When you meet him, you'll know instantly that he likes people and that he enjoys helping them navigate the sometimes-complicated process of buying real estate. As a buyer specialist, Brad works tirelessly for his clients to represent their interests. Licensed to sell in Tennessee and Georgia, Brad works with first time homebuyers, investors, and people relocating to the Chattanooga region. In addition to his work with buyers, Brad also serves as the managing broker of the Hixson, Tennessee office of Keller Williams Realty.

For more information about Cheryl and Brad Fuqua, visit www.TheFuquaGroup.com.

Why a Lender Is a Strategic Participant in Successful Real Estate Transactions

Michelle Noble

Introduction

Michelle Noble is a Residential Mortgage Loan Originator and the Branch Manager for Willow Bend Mortgage in San Antonio, Texas. She helps borrowers arrange residential mortgage financing for home purchases and refinancing in South Texas.

Michelle grew up in a real estate family and got her start in the industry as a real estate agent. After eight years as a top producing agent, she decided to take her comprehensive knowledge of residential and rural property sales in South Texas to the mortgage side of the real estate industry as a loan officer. Michelle has over twenty years of experience in mortgage lending and is the recipient of numerous awards for excellence.

In this chapter Michelle provides an overview of important strategies related to selecting the right lender for a home purchase. Typically, people think in terms of the lender being only relevant to the buyer, or borrower. She also provides insights for sellers and real estate agents who also have a major stake in the buyer's lender selection.

Mortgage Strategies for Buyers

A home is generally the largest asset that individuals or families own and buying a home is generally a very emotional purchase. Even before starting to look for a home, the first step should be getting comfortable with the financial aspects of purchasing a home, like establishing a budget and making sure of the amount of loan you will be able to qualify for. After all, it doesn't make sense to start looking at homes before you really know what you can afford. This is best accomplished by meeting with an experienced loan officer. A loan officer will go through the entire loan process, discuss how much money will be needed for a down payment, appraisal, and other closing costs and the monthly payment. We often hear that people are nervous and hold off on talking with a loan officer because they are uncertain about how the process works. After talking with a loan officer, they usually realize how easy the discussion was and would have started much sooner had they known how easy it really was.

The loan officer will inquire about the amount of money you have available for a down payment, income, existing debts, and other financial parameters to help you understand the amount of loan you are qualified for. If you provide all the financial documentation required for a loan, the loan officer will be able to underwrite the loan and provide a preapproval letter. In this manner your financing abilities will already have been addressed upfront. Final approval will still be subject to an appraisal, property inspections, title work, and a survey after you are under contract to purchase your home.

It's important to understand that preapproval is based on the facts of your financial situation at the time when your documents are reviewed. After you have been preapproved, don't take on any more debt, as that may nullify the preapproval status. It's not the time to go out and buy a new car or borrow to buy furniture for your new home. Job stability is also critical, so this would not be the time to change employment. Life happens, so if something in your financial situation changes between the time you have been qualified and have purchased a home, be sure to discuss it with your loan officer.

Most real estate agents ask that you be preapproved even before showing homes. It's a safety precaution and a service to sellers and their agents. Also, most sellers and their agents will not consider offers that are not backed up with a preapproval letter. Preapproval also gives a buyer peace of mind that they can shop for properties in a specific price range and be comfortable that the financial aspects have already been covered and they will be able to close on the purchase.

Online mortgage companies have become more visible and, on the surface, appear to be a modern approach. They may serve a purpose for tech-savvy people who prefer to do everything for themselves, but we're seeing a big push back with the service levels offered by the technology-driven mortgage companies. There is so much information available on the internet, but it is frequently conflicting, so it's difficult to get all the questions answered online. Most borrowers feel more comfortable meeting with a loan officer that will review their financial situation and help them tailor a loan that best meets their objectives.

Local lenders are generally more likely to take the time to sit down with borrowers, analyze their objectives and situation, and help them select a loan product that's best for them. It's important to know that mortgage companies are like any other type of business. Some loan officers have a great deal of experience and then there are others that are recently licensed that maybe are not as familiar with the guidelines and the nuances of different loan programs. Underwriting guidelines change frequently as well, so it's critical for loan officers to stay up to date on requirements of different loan products that are available. Too often borrowers get turned down for loans that they should be able to qualify for. It's a matter of the experience of the loan officer that reviewed their file.

I'm just as concerned about our loan officers turning down a loan that we actually can do as I am about preapproving a loan that will not get final approval. It takes a thorough understanding the regulatory guidelines for the various types of loans that are available and trying to fit the borrower into a program that will work for them. We try to never tell a client, "No." We will tell them, "Yes, you are ready," or "You're not ready yet." If they are not ready, we will outline the steps they can take so they will be ready and how long it should take. We'll help them develop a plan and work with them until they are at a point where they are able to purchase.

One of the biggest misconceptions among homebuyers is that it takes a 20% down payment to be able to buy a house. Unfortunately, this misunderstanding holds many people back from considering purchasing a home. There are some great programs available for first-time homebuyers with a limited amount of money for a down payment. FHA loans, as one example, have been a traditional solution for first-time homebuyers because the down payment can be as low as 3.5% and the underwriting guidelines are not as stringent. Fannie Mae and Freddie Mac both have programs for first-time homebuyers that require as little as a 3% down payment. In rural areas there is a UDSA loan product that provides up to 100% financing for first-time homebuyers. Note that guidelines change from time-to-time, so these down payment percentages could change in the future.

Most of the loan products feature a fixed interest rate over the life of the loan, which is best for most people. There are also adjustable rate loans programs. Most of the adjustable rate loans have a fixed rate for a specified time, such as for the first three to seven years, and then they adjust annually based on prevailing interest rates, with a cap on the maximum interest rate increase each year and over the life of the loan. The initial rate on the adjustable rate loans is usually a bit lower than on a fixed rate loan, but after the loan starts adjusting it can go higher or lower than what the rate would have been on a fixed rate loan. Adjustable rate loans can be a good choice for someone that knows they will be moving before the rate starts adjusting. As an example, military families that transfer every few years, and know they will be selling when they transfer, might benefit from an adjustable rate loan. Otherwise there is a risk with adjustable rate loans because it's a gamble against higher prevailing rates in the future.

Selecting the right loan officer and mortgage company is an important aspect of a happy and successful home purchase. Of course, you want to work with a reputable company, but the experience level of the loan officer is very important as well. Inquire about the number of years of experience as well as the level of loan production. Do they have a local office where you can meet in person? Are you going to be speaking with the same loan officer throughout the process? Are they willing to take the time to explain the variety of different loan programs and help you find the program that best matches your needs? Our loan officers are all seasoned and usually have at least ten years of experience in the industry.

Mortgage Strategies for Sellers

You're planning on selling your home, but where are you moving after you sell? Sometimes homeowners that are selling their home haven't thought that far ahead and are taking it one step at a time because they believe they have enough time to figure that out after they get a contract on their existing home. Real estate markets change based on the supply and demand and over the past few years we've experienced a fast-paced market where attractive homes sell quickly. If you aren't prepared for the next step, you may not be able to accept an offer and have just wasted time on the market. Before listing your existing home, it's better to be prepared with a plan of what you are going to do after your home sells. Unless you have cash for a new purchase after selling your existing home, you'll need a loan. The best time to start the loan process is before your current home goes on the market.

Simultaneously buying and selling can be a complicated and stressful process. Meeting with a loan officer in advance can help you outline timing and sequencing options that will best work for you. You will find out if you must sell the current home to be able to buy a new one or if you can purchase before selling. If you can purchase in advance, it alleviates the issue of where you're going to live. Regardless of the outcome, you will be well informed on options available to you which makes the entire process easier and less stressful. Much of what I discussed earlier for buyers applies to sellers that are going to purchase another property.

When your home is on the market and you are attracting offers, you will be expecting buyers making offers to have already been preapproved for a loan. They will present a preapproval letter from a lender, but how confident can you be that the lender has done a complete underwriting job or that the lender can get the loan closed on time? One of the largest frustrations for sellers is getting under contract with a buyer, and at the last minute find out that the loan isn't going to be finalized. You may have packed and are ready to move and the buyer's agent calls saying the loan isn't going to close. Unfortunately, this happens a lot. You've taken your home off the market for a few weeks only for the sale to fall apart. I've got a strategy for sellers to virtually eliminate this situation that most real estate agents and homeowners are not aware of.

In our market it is common for the buyer to request concessions from the seller to pay for some of the buyer's closing costs and the seller is allowed to do that. These might include some or all of the following: origination or administrative fee for the loan, appraisal, survey, title charges other than the title policy, flood certificate, and discount points. The amount may be limited to a certain percentage depending on the loan type. The risk reduction strategy is to agree to pay for closing costs, but in return, the seller is going to dictate that the buyer use the seller's preferred lender. This is similar to the situation where a builder can require that if they are going to pay for a title policy, the buyer is going to use the builder's preferred title company. The seller can't dictate who the lender will be, but the seller can decide to offer the concessions only if the preferred lender is used for the transaction.

This strategy is best deployed when the real estate agent has a history of excellent service with a specific experienced loan officer. The introduction of the strategy and the loan officer to the seller usually occurs when the agent is discussing the listing with the seller and talking with them about preparing the home. This concept protects against the buyer stating that they are preapproved through a company that the seller's agent is not familiar with and then having to deal with the risk of the unknown as the transaction is moving toward the closing. This gives a seller peace of mind that the buyer is working with a local lender that has a proven track record of accurate underwriting and that gets their loans closed on time.

Mortgage Strategies for Real Estate Agents

Before entering the mortgage industry, I was a real estate agent. I quickly learned that selecting the right loan officer to partner with is one of the most important decisions an agent can make. It's one thing to get to the contract stage, but too many home sales fall through because the lender didn't properly underwrite during the preapproval process or they couldn't get the loan closed on time. Real estate agents should develop an informal team with an experienced loan officer, so they can work closely together to eliminate most of the issues that can come up during a transaction.

The agent can handle the entire real estate side of the transaction and know that they don't have to worry about the details of loan guidelines or processing the loan. The agent can feel comfortable introducing their clients to a true professional who can help them get preapproved and their loans closed. It's a partnership with a constant flow of communication between the agent and loan officer whose goals are the same—to work together to close the transaction, keep the clients happy, and retain them as lifelong customers.

Most real estate agents depend on a having qualified buyers to sell homes and earn a commission. If you are getting feedback that your preferred lender is not able to get a loan done for some of your clients, it limits your ability to serve some people. Agents will get a second opinion on a $250 air conditioner repair, but generally not when a lender doesn't want to approve a loan. Why not seek out another loan officer and get a second opinion on loan qualification? As confident as I am in my experience and in the experience of the loan officers that work with me, we do not turn down a borrower unless a loan officer and a management team member have looked at that loan. It's interesting that a meaningful percentage of loans that I close have been turned down by another lender when I am providing the second opinion.

Earlier, I discussed a strategy for sellers that significantly reduces the risk that a buyer for their property can't get their loan closed. This concept is particularly useful for listing agents, because one of the most common reasons that deals fall apart is the buyer's loan doesn't get funded. What if you could choose the lender for the buyer of your listing customer's home and know that the lender is well qualified to underwrite and close? You or your seller can't insist on a certain lender; however, you can make the choice of a lender you choose very attractive to a buyer. It's very common in our market for the seller to agree to concessions paying for some of the buyer's closing costs. This is probably something listing agents should discuss upfront with their clients, so they know what to expect at the negotiation stage. Instead of looking at the potential concessions as a negative, let's consider a way to structure anticipated concessions to gain something from the buyer. A strategy that I have found to work well is to identify that certain closing costs of the buyer will be paid by the seller, but only if the buyer uses a lender specified by the seller. Due to the financial benefit of the concessions, buyers are likely to agree to use the preferred lender. Now, the seller and agent can much better control the likelihood of accurate loan underwriting and being able to get the loan closed.

Selecting the Right Lender

Whether you are a buyer, a seller, or a real estate agent, a successful real estate transaction depends on the buyer being able to get a mortgage funded on time, unless the buyer is paying all cash for the purchase. One of the biggest frustrations for all the parties to a home sale is approaching the closing date and only then discovering that the buyer is not going to be able to get the loan. Working with an experienced loan officer that has a reputation for properly underwriting loans and getting them closed on time significantly reduces the risk.

Important factors to check that can indicate experience as well as service level:

- Years of experience as a loan officer.
- Level of loan production.
- Online reviews and testimonials.
- Client references.
- Is there a local office where you can meet in person?
- Will you be working with the same person throughout the process or get passed off to different people at different stages?
- Will they compete a thorough review and underwriting of your documents, so a preapproval is meaningful?
- Are they willing to listen to your goals, go over the entire process in advance, and explain the variety of loan programs available so you can understand the best fit for your specific needs?
- How will they be communicating with you during the process?

What Clients Are Saying

"Michelle was extremely helpful in the home buying process. Everything went smoothly and I was able to get the home I wanted without any issues. I would definitely go to Michelle again in the future."

—Kayla B.

"Mortgage made easy. I would definitely recommended her to all of my clients. Thank you for making a difficult time so easy to get through. It felt like I was working with family."

—Merideth G.

"Michelle is very friendly and patient. She will take the time to answer any questions or concerns you may have. I will highly recommend Michelle with my family and friends for future mortgage needs. Outstanding delivery on my mortgage needs."

—Brodie H.

"Michelle fought for me from the initial signing of the contract to closing. She was a PIT BULL! I wouldn't recommend anyone else to fight in my corner."

—Christy C.

"Michelle Noble made buying a home easy. She answered all our questions and concerns in a timely fashion. She went above and beyond to insure our transaction went smoothly! We are pleased with our purchase and her team!"

—Angela P.

"Michelle was fantastic to work with. She understood our unique situation and always kept us in the loop of what was going on with our loan. Michelle is very responsive to emails and phone calls and shared the same sense of urgency to close as we did."

—Misty M.

About Michelle Noble

Michelle Noble helps borrowers arrange residential mortgage financing for home purchases and refinancing in South Texas. She is the Branch Manager and a Residential Mortgage Loan Originator at Willow Bend Mortgage in San Antonio, Texas. Michelle started her career as a real estate agent at the age of nineteen and rapidly became a top producer. After eight years as an agent with a strong knowledge of residential and rural property sales in South Texas, she decided to move over to the lending side as a mortgage loan officer. She has over twenty years of experience originating mortgages and helping borrowers achieve their dream of home ownership.

Michelle is a member of the San Antonio Board of Realtors® and the Texas Association of Realtors®. She has the Mortgage Lending Seal of Integrity, is a Certified Veteran and Military Housing Specialist, and Graduate, REALTOR® Institute (GRI). Michelle has been the recipient of several awards including the Texas Monthly "Five Star Customer Service Award," "President's Club," and "Expert Network Award." She has been featured in several national magazines including Forbes, Entrepreneur, The Oprah Magazine, Top Agent, and Texas Monthly.

NMLS# 199832

For more information about Michelle Noble, visit http://www.MNobleLoans.com.

Strategies for Buying or Selling a Home Under Different Market Conditions

Paul George

Introduction

Paul George grew up working in his family's grocery store business, starting at an early age. He was always around customers and learned how to communicate with adults from his father, who also demonstrated a great work ethic. After graduating from Ohio State University with a marketing degree, Paul was expecting to be running small grocery stores in the family business, but he got interested in selling real estate. Although he was initially interested in the commercial real estate field, the economy was slow, and the residential market showed more promise at the time. Paul started his residential real estate practice in 1991 and hasn't looked back since.

Paul is affiliated with Keller Williams Greater Columbus Realty. He helps buyers and sellers in the Columbus,

Ohio area with their residential real estate transactions. He primarily works with referrals from past clients and has helped generations of families buy or sell their homes.

Residential real estate market conditions and trends change in cycles based on national and local factors. Paul has experienced multiple cycles during his real estate career and in this chapter provides strategies and insights for buyers and sellers based on different market conditions.

Defining the Market

We'll be discussing strategies for residential real estate buyers and sellers that differ based on prevailing market conditions. We generally define the type of market based on the relative balance in supply and demand for homes in the local market. National economic conditions, such as the state of the economy, unemployment rates, and interest rates play a big role on the demand side, but real estate is always a very local market. In the greater Columbus area, and generally in other markets around the country, we consider the real estate market to be balanced when there is a 6.5-month supply of available homes for sale. When the supply is less than 6.5 months, sellers may have more leverage and it is considered a "seller's market." With demand exceeding supply in a seller's market, sellers are in a relatively stronger position in negotiating the terms and conditions of the sale and are less likely to reduce the price or offer concessions. On the other hand, a period where there is more than a 6.5-month supply is considered a "buyer's market." In a buyer's market, buyers generally have more leverage on their side and are usually negotiating more on the price and trying to request concessions. It's important to understand the market situation because strategies to maximize the net price for a seller or obtain the best deal for a buyer vary depending on market condition.

Selling in a Seller's Market

The inventory of available homes is low by historical standards in a seller's market. This creates a dilemma for homeowners that have an interest in moving. Where will you buy and move to when you sell? It can become a vicious cycle where fewer homeowners want to sell because of the difficulty in finding a new home. As a result, many homeowners that desire to move just throw up their hands and say, "I'm not going to sell."

Depending on your financial circumstances, there are some solutions that can help in a tight market. Although it can be cost prohibitive for some people, moving to a short-term rental property after closing the sale of your home is one option. This removes the pressure to immediately find a suitable new home. Of course, you have to move two times, but if getting into a new home or moving to a certain neighborhood or district is critical, this is one way to make it happen.

Lenders are starting to adjust to market realities and have been more accommodating with creative solutions like bridge loans for homeowners. Using a bridge loan, a homeowner can find and close on a new home first and then put their existing home up for sale. In a strong market, they can be pretty confident that their house is going to sell in a reasonable time. Lenders have made the process more affordable by combining the underwriting for the bridge loan and the permanent financing, and the borrower only has to pay once for the credit reports and appraisals.

When selling a home, the usual advice is to have any issues repaired and make appropriate updates to the home. In a tight market, sellers have a bit more flexibility since demand exceeds supply, and the home is more likely to sell, even if everything is not perfect. You always need to present a very clean and un-cluttered home, but you may not have to replace old carpeting, repaint, or update the furnaces and the air conditioning systems. Of course, every situation is unique and an experienced agent can advise on the best route to take to maximize the net profit on the sale. Sometimes in a seller's market it can be more profitable to make certain updates such as granite countertops or flooring as that can help sell the home for a premium and generate a bidding war among buyers. I want to point out that the home presentation necessary to attract buyers does differ based on the price range of the home. Buyers looking at mid-range or average price range homes in a very tight market may put up with a lot more flaws than buyers considering higher priced, or luxury homes. There is rarely a true seller's market for luxury homes, even when the overall market has limited inventory.

Even in a seller's market, the price needs to be set correctly. The market will give us feedback if the pricing is off. If there are limited or no showings in the first couple of weeks and no offers, it's pretty easy to say the pricing is off. On the other hand, if we have multiple offers and potential buyers are bidding the price up, we are in a strong position and may be able to negotiate the price even higher. One caveat to accepting offers at higher than the list price is the typical appraisal contingency that lets the buyer walk if the appraisal doesn't substantiate the value. This is an area where we may be able to negotiate the contingency away if the buyer is committed to purchasing the home and has the funds necessary to close the gap if the lender limits the loan amount due to the appraisal.

In a seller's market, some homeowners may believe that they don't need an agent to help them sell their home. The reality is that experienced real estate agents are professionals in what they do and selling at the highest price, netting the most for the seller, and in the shortest time is usually accomplished by working with an experienced agent. An agent is going to advise on the market value and the steps to take in preparation and presentation to maximize the net profit, help vet the buyer's financing pre-approval to gain confidence on the buyer's and lender's ability to close the loan on time and handle any objections from home inspectors.

When selling a home without an agent, sellers tend to just choose the highest offer and expect that the buyer is going to be able to close the transaction. The reality is that not all loan pre-qualifications are equal, and some lenders have a good reputation for underwriting and following through, while others don't have a history of meeting the appraisal or closing deadlines. Local lenders tend to be better able to handle the financing in a timely manner and know the local customs as apply to title insurance and common closing costs. Online lenders and some national banks may not be attuned to the local situation and may not be forthcoming in providing details about the strength of a pre-qualification to a seller. A big mistake is signing a purchase contract with a buyer whose lender may not be able to close and then having your home off the market for a few weeks only to find out the transaction is not going to close.

If you are trying to sell your home yourself, who will hold the earnest money? Lenders don't want to see the seller holding the money, so that's another complication. Dealing with objections on home inspections can be another challenge for sellers and not an easy conversation to have. It's not unusual for a seller to take negative findings personally and start down the path of an adversarial type of relationship instead of one where you work together to solve the challenge. An agent can be a great buffer, negotiating a solution on your behalf.

Of course, even in a hot market, exposure to a wide range of buyers is important to get the highest and best offers. When you attract more people to a listing, there is a much greater opportunity to get buyers competing against each other and bidding the price up. If you do it yourself, you're relying on a much smaller group of people that happen to drive by or happen to see an ad. Experienced agents have so many more resources and are always networking with other agents who have ready, willing, and able buyers, so the actual quantity of people that will see the listing is much greater.

Buying in a Seller's Market

In a seller's market, buyers are competing with each other for the most attractive properties, so preparation and mindset to move quickly are critical to success. Commonly buyers are feeling that they need to buy something because they have missed out on other homes they wanted. There's more of a chance of buyer's remorse when settling on a purchase, just to make sure you buy something, but a good agent will prevent this from happening.

Financing pre-approval must be solid and needs to be arranged in advance of seriously looking at homes. Sellers are not going to waste their time and take their home off the market unless there is a solid pre-approval letter in place from a lender well known to be able to underwrite and close on time. If you are looking at homes and see the one you want, you're likely too late if your financing hasn't already been lined up. When working with a buyer, I want the lender to be open to calling listing agents to vouch for the buyer's pre-approval and to discuss the buyer' solid qualification, so the buyer's offer will be seriously considered.

With lots of competition for the most attractive homes, be prepared to move fast with an offer when you find the ideal home. If you spend too much time thinking about it, another buyer may come in and buy it before you have made an offer. You may even need to offer more than the listing price. Frequently, sellers have unique objectives and I try to get as much information as possible from the seller's agent so we can address concerns in the offer. Sometimes the seller has special needs around the closing timing or may need to retain possession for a time after the closing. If we can glean this insight from the seller's agent, we may be able to tailor an offer that best matches the seller's needs. You also may need to forego requesting a home warranty or requesting an appraisal contingency if the market is hot.

Although price is almost always the primary seller concern, proper presentation of a buyer can reinforce the buyer's position when a seller has to make a choice among different offers. Sometimes emotions come into play, so I always recommend that my buyers write a personal letter about themselves, including a picture and the reasons why they like the home. Discussing in detail about features you like about the home and how it is the perfect fit for you can impress the sellers that you really like their tastes and helps connect with the seller on an emotional level. Sometimes an emotional letter helps the buyer reach the tipping point that gets their offer preferred over the others.

Selling in a Buyer's Market

In a buyer's market, sellers have a lot of competition for the sale, so making the home stand out as among the best on the market will help it sell faster. Compared to being in a seller's market, the leverage is totally switched around and sellers need to do a lot more preparation before putting their home on the market.

It's critical that the home be in good condition and that all of the systems and appliances are in working order. When buyers have lots of choices, they don't want to deal with a home that is in needs of repairs, and for the most part they don't want to spend time or money after purchasing to make repairs. Buyers are going to have the home inspected after a contract is signed, so it's better to know in advance what kind of issues are going to arise. Getting your home pre-inspected before it goes on the market can uncover unseen issues that will likely be discovered later that could even make a buyer back out of the contract. Addressing issues found in a pre-inspection early can head off the problems later. You may even want to show the pre-inspection report to potential buyers indicating how issues were remedied. Sometimes this may even result in a buyer deciding not to include an inspection contingency or a shorter inspection contingency period. I foresee that we may get to a point where pre-inspections become routine in the industry, although there are no present state standards for home inspectors.

Many people enjoy watching the TV shows on home improvement and they are expecting to see updates and upgrades like they are used to seeing on TV and in magazines, especially in a buyer's market. They're going to want to see colors that match current trends and tastes, not something in style decades ago. As a seller, you need to match as best as possible buyer expectations. If you are working with me, I'll walk through your home and provide a list of things that need to be done to get the home ready to sell. Of course, we will work with you on a budget that you can afford and recommend only changes that will net you more on your sale.

We want to make a good first impression, so the home needs to be thoroughly cleaned and organized. The landscaping should be tidy as well. Most people have accumulated lots of personal items over the years that are on full display in their home. This can be a big distraction for buyers, looking at the pictures online as well as during in-person showings. They tend to focus on all the stuff, instead of the home, itself. You are going to be moving anyway, so pack up what you don't need and store it away until you move. If the home or certain rooms are crowded with furniture, consider removal of some of the furniture to open the home up. A de-cluttered, organized home looks more spacious to visitors.

Make sure you are prepared for showings. The home needs to be as clean and tidy for showings as possible. Lights should be on and blinds open to let in the natural light. Light music in the background and pleasant smells make the environment more attractive for visitors.

Incentives may also help put your home into a more competitive situation. Things like paying for some of the buyer's closing costs, including an extended home warranty, or a club or gym membership might attract more buyers. Some types of incentives, such as a new TV or an automobile, are not allowed by lenders, so you must be careful in selecting appropriate incentives.

A great way to give potential buyers a better feel for what it's like living in the home and in the neighborhood, is to write a letter to buyers. This isn't meant to discuss features they can see while touring your home or looking at pictures. It's intended to convey benefits of living there including the friendly neighbors, how much you have enjoyed the informal neighborhood gatherings and activities, nearby amenities, and other aspects of the area. This is a way to create an emotional bond to the property.

An often-overlooked aspect of selling a home is to review the feedback from potential buyers through their agents. Whenever a buyer tours the home, we reach out to the buyer's agent to get feedback on any objections and then we address overcoming the issues. It could be people saying that the home smells like a cat. In this case, we need to do something. Sometimes it's really ugly wallpaper in one room and multiple people are making comments on it. Unfortunately, most buyers don't have a lot of imagination and don't see the ease of replacing the wallpaper, so it's much better to address the issue by removing the wallpaper and painting a neutral color. Sometimes we need to do a little research to uncover issues. If we review the hits on our online listing and see lots of hits, but we are not getting any showings, there's something not appealing to buyers. It could be something in the photos. As an example, maybe you have a bright red wall that is sticking out like a sore thumb. In this case we would suggest painting it a neutral color. If we receive repeated feedback with pricing objections when buyers are comparing our listing with other similar homes they have seen, we may need to adjust the price to attract buyers.

Buying in a Buyer's Market

In a buyer's market, the supply of homes for sale is greater than the demand, so buyers hold more leverage and they don't have to feel that pressure of finding and buying a house right at the moment. They can actually take more time and think about it a little bit, and in the end have a better opportunity to get a better deal.

I like to first understand the seller's situation and true motivation. How long has the home sat on the market? What does the seller owe? What is my assessment of the true market value? This is a chance to use the buyer's leverage to make a lower than normal offer, improve the terms and conditions in the buyer's favor, or request higher incentives from the seller in terms of a better home warranty or covering the buyer's closing costs.

With a good supply of attractive homes on the market and with time on their side, buyers should always be willing to walk away if they can't finalize a favorable deal.

Selling in a Balanced Market

In a balanced market, sellers need to be aware that it may take two or three months for a sale and preparation is key. Follow the guidelines for preparation in a buyer's market, because a clean, attractive home is going to sell faster than other similarly priced homes, all other things being equal. Expect a stream of showings while the home is listed. It may be two or three a week or maybe five on a weekend. Accommodate showings as much as possible. Most people in a balanced market will give you a day or two notice for a showing but be prepared for showings on short notice as well. In a neighborhood where there are two or three other houses for sale, it's not uncommon that buyers will request to see your home when they look at the others, even if their agent didn't tell them about your house n advance. It's better to show a house on short notice and apologize later for it not looking perfect than to miss a showing. Be prepared to take pets with you and to put the laundry in a basket and put them in your car.

Buying in a Balanced Market

In a balanced market there is a good inventory of homes available, so you don't generally have to jump to make an immediate offer on a home that you want, as other homes will probably be available if you miss the first one. You have more time to make a decision and sellers may be open to offers below the listing price.

It's still important to make yourself as attractive as you can as a buyer. Getting your financing pre-approval as discussed earlier is still important, because sellers want to make sure they are negotiating with people who have the ability to close. I also recommend that you write a letter to the sellers to present with offers as discussed in the section about buying in a seller's market. At the end of the day, the better you present yourself as a buyer, usually the better position you are in with respect to negotiating the best possible deal.

Selecting the Best Agent for You

A home is one of the most valuable assets of a family or an individual. When choosing a real estate agent, it's important to pick one that has the experience that can guide you through the process and one that you can trust will always be representing your best interests. An experienced agent will be an "insider," who is familiar with all aspects of the transaction. Buying or selling a home can be an intense time with frequent communications, so make sure that you have a compatible personality with the agent you choose. Try to find out about the agent and the experience other clients have had with the agent. Referrals from satisfied clients are some of the strongest indicators of a good agent. Look at the experience level in years of experience in the industry and number of successfully completed transactions. Has the agent been through a number of market cycles? Knowledge of strategies to make the best deal for clients based on local market conditions is a major asset. Is the agent willing to share his or her knowledge with clients?

If you are selling your home, look at the agent's past marketing campaigns and how the homes were presented and marketed. Is the agent willing to spend money on effective marketing?

The role of an agent for buyers has evolved as more information is readily available online, so we aren't just finding homes for buyers. Our role is to make sure buyers understand the details about various communities where they have an interest and assist them get through the transaction and all of the lender requirements. This includes having a vetted list of home inspectors and other vendors that are needed during and after the transaction.

What Clients Are Saying

"Paul not only helped sell our house but also helped my Brother, Sister and Sister in laws Parents"

—Patrick & Amy M.

"It Almost Seemed as if Paul would not let me buy a house, he made me be patient, I'm glad we waited, we finally found the right one, Thanks Paul"

—Michelle L.

"Paul showed us numerous homes and we finally figured out we had to build, he helped us through the whole process from choices for resale to helping with our punchout list."

—Elizabeth C. & Stephan B.

"Our Father passed away suddenly and Paul helped coordinate the disposal of the contents, the title process and finally the sale"

—Adam, Mike & Kaitlyn F.

"After Paul sold us our house, he helped us challenge our property taxes, he helped us save $1200 a year on our property taxes"

—Doug & Amber G.

About Paul George

Paul George is the leader of the Paul George Group, affiliated with Keller Williams Greater Columbus Realty in Columbus, Ohio. He has been a residential real estate agent since 1991 and has successfully navigated buyers and sellers through real estate transactions in a number of market cycles.

Paul graduated with a marketing degree from Ohio State University. He is a member of multiple local and national Realtor® boards. Paul has won a number of awards for sales excellence and sales volume and is among the top 2% of all real estate agents and brokers in sales volume in the greater Columbus area.

Paul enjoys being an educator and advocate for client success. He has authored a number of articles and blogs on real estate strategies as they relate to different market conditions. He is frequently quoted in local newspapers as an expert on real estate trends and has appeared on radio talk shows discussing real estate strategies.

Paul is a native and lifelong resident of the Columbus area. He is married to Linda and they have two sons. Paul is a volunteer baseball and basketball coach and for the past 20 plus years has been a volunteer at Kobacker House, a local hospice facility.

For more information about Paul George, visit http://www.HalfTheBeatles.KW.com.

.

Buying and Selling Homes in the Cincinnati Area

Scott Oyler

Introduction

Scott Oyler and the Oyler Group help buyers and sellers in the greater Cincinnati, Ohio area that includes Northern Kentucky. Scott and his team work with sellers that are moving up to their next home on both the selling and buying side. They also enjoy working with first time homebuyers and people relocating into the area. Scott and his team are affiliated with Coldwell Banker West Shell in Cincinnati.

Scott's family has a long history in real estate in the Cincinnati area. His grandfather owned an agency that was purchased by Coldwell Banker in the 1980s and his father has been involved on the management side of Coldwell Banker for many years. Scott started his career in commercial real estate after college, selling apartment communities. He decided to change his focus to the residential side representing buyers and sellers over eight years ago. Scott consistently achieves high sales performance and has won a number of awards for sales excellence.

In this chapter, Scott provides insights for buyers and sellers in the greater Cincinnati area.

Selling Your Cincinnati Area Home

Most homeowners have an emotional connection to their home, and it can be a difficult decision to sell. They've likely celebrated many events over the years there and they have decorated it with their style and tastes. When you've made the decision to sell, it's best to emotionally detach so that you can move forward in preparing the home for sale. You almost have to think of the house as no longer your own and make it appeal to the widest possible audience of buyers. It certainly can be difficult, but the best mindset is to think of your house as a product, making it as marketable as possible.

Pricing the home correctly is one of the most critical aspects of selling. It's important to consider that the seller controls the listing price but the market determines the actual selling price. It's related to market conditions, like supply and demand, and comparisons to other properties that have recently sold or that are currently on the market. We start with comparable sales in the recent past few months. This gives us a base range to start with. We know the exact sale prices along with details of those homes, like square footage, number of bedrooms, baths, and other important characteristics. We also look at active listings, because these are going to be the competition for your home. If there's not a lot of competition, then maybe you can price on the higher end of the estimated market value range. On the other hand, if there are several fairly similar homes available, especially in the same subdivision, you should make sure that your home is positioned as one of the best values among the competition.

Along with establishing a realistic price, preparation for sale is the most important aspect of selling a home for the highest price. The first step is to assess if repairs are needed and get them fixed in advance of going on the market. Obviously, systems and appliances need to be in good working condition. Look around the exterior to see if any paint needs to be touched up, or if there are any signs of damage to the roof, gutters, and other parts of the house. Once your home is under contract, the buyer will be ordering inspections, and if a number of different issues show up, it can scare them. Remember that potential buyers are going to be making judgments about how well the home has been maintained and even simple things matter. Replace burned out light bulbs, install a battery in chirpy smoke detectors, and fix any cosmetic issues.

First impressions are critical because buyers are making decisions on the home in the first few seconds. It may be online looking at photos. They will be making a quick decision on whether they want to go ahead and take the next step to set up a showing. If they are at the home for a showing, it's the first impression as they get out of the car and walk up to your front door that is so important. We want to create a great "curb appeal," so the feeling is very positive right from the start. Freshen up the landscaping, particularly in the front yard. This can be difficult in the Cincinnati area in the winter, but for the most part, the exterior should be looking good. Is the front door, itself, presenting well? If the paint or stain is old or fading, a fresh coat will make it pop.

To appeal to the most buyers, we want to neutralize the interior as much as possible. Bright or loud colors can be a turnoff to many people, so repaint with neutral color tones. Most people have collected lots of personal items and decorations over time that are on display on the walls or shelves. We want buyers to focus on the home, not the personal items, as they are walking through the home or looking at pictures online. Removal of most of these personal items will let people see the home and also give the impression of more space. If countertops, shelves, and walls are cluttered, buyers will have a hard time imagining living in the home or even having enough room for their possessions. You'll be packing and moving anyway, so pack up these things in advance and eliminate the clutter. Buyers will also be looking at the amount of closet space, and there never seems to be enough. Pack up clothes you won't be using while the home is on the market and organize everything neatly on bars and racks. When someone looks in a closet there should be an impression of some empty space.

Look at the furniture arrangement. Are there adequate pathways so people can easily walk through the home, or is it crowded? Staging the furniture by removing some, or rearranging pieces can make a big difference from a buyer's perspective. Again, if the home is crowded, it looks smaller and buyers may get the impression that their furniture will not fit. Removing just one or two pieces from a bedroom may open it up and provide a sense of space.

There may be quite a few tasks to complete before the home is ready for the market. I recommend getting it in "picture-perfect" shape rather than rush it to market, even if it means a delay. Typically, the most buyer traffic, both online and in person with showings, is going to be right after the listing is active. The home should be presented in the best possible light right from the time it goes on the market. Our work in shooting photos, finalizing the description, and getting all of the marketing materials produced will also be done in advance of the listing, so that the home and the presentation stands out among the competition as the listing goes live.

Another technique that I recommend to my clients is to write a letter to potential buyers that describes what it's like living in the home and the neighborhood. It will include the many reasons why they have enjoyed living there and make it very personable so people seeing the letter get a good feel for the neighborhood. It can include some information on how great the neighbors are, fun neighborhood events, nearby amenities people enjoy, and even can talk about resources in the neighborhood for babysitting. The letter can be left on the kitchen countertop so buyers can see it as they are viewing the home.

Great photography is critical in presenting a home online, so once it's show-ready we capture the elegance with professional photography. Our photographers are skilled in capturing the home in the best lighting and from the best angles to display the depth and space. If there are big selling features like a phenomenal yard or beautiful adjacent open space we will also use a video. There is no better way to tell a story of special exterior features than with overhead videos shot with a drone.

The attention span for buyers looking at online listings is not very long as they are flipping through listings. We need to capture their attention in a few seconds, at most.

We organize the photos so that the absolute best three or four show up first. If the first few photos attract attention, there's a better chance that buyers will continue through the rest of the photos and read the written description details.

When everything is ready, the home is listed on the local multiple listing service and also on the major national web portals like, Zillow, Realtor.com, and Trulia. We want to be where people are looking, so social media is a big part of a successful marketing campaign now. We use a lot of Facebook ads to get the home in front of as many target buyers as possible.

Neighbors can be a great resource for finding buyers. They may have friends or relatives interested in buying a home, and possibly interested in moving into your neighborhood. Another strategy we use is notifying neighbors and people in nearby neighborhoods of the new listing. One way to accomplish this is to post the home on neighborhood Facebook groups that are focused on specific neighborhoods in close proximity to the home. We also send out postcards to residents in the neighborhood informing them of the listing.

I talked about making sure everything is ready before listing the home, but depending on market conditions we may also start with some online pre-marketing to create some extra demand even before the home is officially on the market. We post the home as "coming soon," and just provide a sneak peek online, without official in person showings. With this strategy we try to generate excitement and desire to see the home the first day it's on the market.

Unique properties can also benefit from placements in publications. If there is a good story behind the home, we may be able to get the story picked up in local publications.

I like to have listings go live on a Thursday or a Friday so we will have initial buyer traffic over the weekend. At this stage you need to be prepared for showings, especially over that first weekend. You'll need to leave your home during showings, so get prepared to be able to take children and pets with you on short notice. One of the largest mistakes is not making the home accessible for buyers to tour on their schedule. If they can't see your home, they will be looking at others, and they may fall in love with another home and write up an offer before they even have a chance to see yours. That's just a lost opportunity to sell your home.

The home needs to be kept in show-ready condition, so it looks just like a model home as buyers are walking through it. This means keeping it very clean and freshly vacuumed. All of the crumbs need to be picked up from breakfast and no dirty dishes left out. Odors from cooking or from pets can be a problem, so it's important to remove sources of odors as much as you can.

In a fast-moving market we should be getting showings and maybe offers within a week or two. A good rule-of-thumb, though, is to evaluate where we are after two weeks. If we have people walking through the home but no offers at that point, we need to reevaluate the positioning. The most common obstacles are the price or the condition that is causing a lack of offers. The most effective diagnostic approach is to get back feedback from the buyers' agents after their clients have toured the home. What did their clients like and not like about the home? How did the value compare to other homes they toured? If their client selected another home, what were the differences and why did our listing not appear to show as much value? Armed with this kind of information we are ready to recommend some repositioning of the home, if appropriate, adjusting the price or improving the condition. We also need to stay on top of the market. Changing competition may also dictate a need to reposition. As an example, if a couple of new similar listings pop up in the neighborhood, competition is increasing, and we may need to adjust to respond.

As you start receiving offers, it's important to realize that offers are all different and price isn't the only key factor. First and foremost, you want to make sure the buyer is pre-approved for financing and has the ability to close on the home. Getting to an agreement with a non-qualified buyer just takes your home off the market, and you miss out on other opportunities. Buyers may request concessions, such as help with paying closing costs, or a home warranty, or paying for title insurance. Focus on the net price, not just the gross price in the offer.

Your position in the ability to negotiate depends considerably on the market situation. In a seller's market when we are attracting multiple offers, the seller can be more aggressive and dictate more of the terms. You can ask competing buyers to submit their highest and best offer and make them aware of terms that are important to you. These might include the closing timeline, occupancy after closing, and minimization of contingency periods. While a 10-day contingency period for inspections is typical in the area, we may request a 7-day period. An experienced agent will help you through the negotiations and navigate you through to the closing.

A home is one of the largest assets for most individuals or families. Selling your home for the highest amount requires attention to a number of factors, including getting it in the best possible condition so it will present well and setting an appropriate price. It also needs to be marketed professionally with strategies that expose it widely to potential buyers.

Buying Your Cincinnati Area Home

Buying a home is a major life and financial event. First, you should clarify what you are looking for in a home. Of course, defining a budget for the home is important, but also think through all of your expectations in a home. We like to have an initial counseling session with a homebuyer to help them crystalize their objectives in buying a home. We discuss things like desired locations or neighborhoods, size of home and yard, number of bedrooms and baths, commute to work, school preferences, and then work with the client put together a list of needs and wants. We discuss the steps that are involved in buying a home. This is particularly important for a first-time homebuyer. We also review the costs that are likely to be involved for inspections, an appraisal, and other closing costs.

Before starting to look for a home, you need to know the price of a home you can afford as well as get comfortable with the monthly payment. Unless you're paying all cash, you need to get pre-approved for a mortgage to know the amount of loan you can qualify for. If you haven't already been pre-approved, we have mortgage partners that can help you determine your buying range with confidence and that can get the financing closed on time. One of the largest challenges we observe for buyers is that they start the home buying process thinking they can buy a certain price home and later find out they cannot afford it.

Then they have to move the budget down, making it even harder, because then they're comparing houses to the nicer ones that were priced higher. Also, be aware that sellers are not likely to respond to offers that are not backed by a pre-approval. Especially in a competitive market, sellers don't want to get into a contract and take their home off the market with a buyer that may not be able to close with a high degree of certainty.

When buying a home, consider who is going to be representing you in the transaction. One of the biggest mistakes is starting to look at homes on one of the real estate portals like Zillow or Realtor.com and then reaching out to the listing agent to show it. The listing agent represents the seller and will be negotiating on behalf of the seller. As a buyer, you should have your own agent that is representing you, looking out for your best interests, and negotiating on your behalf. This is particularly true for first time homebuyers as a buyer's agent will be your advocate and guide you all the way through the process. A common misconception is that having your own buyer's agent will cost end up costing more. This is not true because the seller will be paying the commission on both the buying and selling side. I should point out that there could be a dual agency arrangement where one agent represents both the seller and the buyer; however, this works best when the buyer is well versed in negotiating skills and understands the process well.

Most home for sale can be found online, but many times the portals can be behind and the information may not be up to date. An active and experienced buyer's agent can help you more aggressively find homes on the market that best meet your needs and is able to network with other agents and get a heads up on properties coming to market before showing up online. You may also skip over some homes that aren't presented well online that still may match your requirements.

Most local buyers have a pretty good knowledge of locations and even specific neighborhoods that will work for them. People relocating to a new area have more of a challenge determining where they should be looking. Online resources are available that can help narrow down the search area, but a neighborhood tour really helps get a feel for the various neighborhoods. We'll schedule a tour of one or two houses for sale in a few candidate neighborhoods. These aren't necessarily the homes you will focus on when we get a little more serious in the search, but you can get an understanding of how prices, amenities, and lifestyle vary by the different communities. You can fairly quickly narrow the search down to two or three neighborhoods that will best match your objectives, and we can then identify all the homes for sale that you should consider and set up showings.

When you have found the ideal home, it's time to craft an offer. What about the price? In determining a fair price, we study comparables, similar homes that have recently sold. We also need to consider market conditions. Is the market appreciating? What is the supply of available homes? Is the supply growing or shrinking? Are listings receiving multiple offers? How long has the home been listed? All of this information will guide us toward an appropriate offer price. If the home is just new to market and homes are selling quickly, you'll have to be more aggressive on the price. If the home has been on the market for a longer time, say 120 days, you may be able to come in a little lower on the offer. I would caution against making low-ball offers, unless the property is clearly overpriced and has lingered on the market. You don't want to offend the seller and low-ball offers may not even generate a response.

Generally, your offer, and the purchase contract, should include certain contingencies. A 10-day inspection period contingency is typical in the local market. Most of the time we will include an appraisal contingency to make sure there's an out if the home doesn't appraise for the purchase price. Also, we include a financing contingency to make sure that the sale is contingent upon you finalizing the mortgage financing. First time homebuyers may also consider asking for a home warranty if the seller hasn't already included one. You saved up a lot of money for your down payment and a home warranty can protect you if a major appliances or system fails in the first year.

In a competitive market where listings are generating multiple offers, we need to pay close attention. Obviously, the price to offer is critical, but the other terms may be important to the seller as well. In this case a "clean" offer, maybe not asking for concessions, like help with closing costs or a home warranty, will make your offer stand out. You can also put down additional earnest money to let the seller know you are a serious buyer.

After an agreement is signed, it's important to rapidly get inspections completed within the contingency period. A general home inspection and termite inspection are most common. If the general home inspection indicates major system or structural issues, the inspector will usually recommend additional specific inspections. Radon gas is somewhat prevalent in the Ohio Valley, and I typically recommend a radon test as well. Although radon mitigation systems cost about $900 to $1,200, depending on the house, it's good to know the situation when you're buying, because when it comes time to sell, the buyer at that time likely will be testing for radon. In older neighborhoods, closer to the urban core and downtown Cincinnati, there may be clay sewer pipes that are more prone to failure. In this case, I suggest having the sewer scoped to determine if there are any cracks or tree roots likely to cause failure of the sewer pipe.

Purchasing a home can be a complex process. An experienced agent can help you find and negotiate the best price and terms for your ideal home while minimizing the stress.

Selecting the Best Agent for You

Buying or selling a home is a major life event for most people. It's also a major financial transaction, so working with an expert is more likely to result in a satisfactory experience. Whether you are buying or selling a home, the agent you choose should have experience in the area where your home is located or where you are interested in purchasing. Timely communications are essential during the buying or selling process, so I recommend working with a full-time agent that will be accessible.

Inquire about the agent's working style and resources. Does the agent work alone, or is there a team supporting the agent? If there is a team, who will you be communicating with and what are the various roles of the team members? A team provides a number of advantages. One is to provide backup if one person is not immediately available.

If you are selling your home, look at how the agent is presenting listings online. Does the photography look professional? Does the online listing give a good first impression? Does the agent appear to have a budget for marketing the home? What marketing channels are used?

As a buyer, and you know the area where you want to purchase a home, does the agent have a good level of experience in that specific area? You're best served by an agent that knows the immediate area, who keeps on top of values and micro trends, and can lead you to the best opportunities.

Level of volume of sales activity is a good indicator of success. Not only total sales over their career, but recent annual sales volume are important. Look at reviews to see if there is a consistent level of client satisfaction. Ask the agent for references and check some of them to find out if prior clients had a good overall experience.

What Clients Are Saying

"I would recommend the Oyler Group in a heartbeat to anyone I know. Scott & his team completely surpassed our expectations. They helped us get a great deal on our dream home and also sell our existing house in 3 days at 100% of list price in Madeira. Having three agents with different responsibilities meant that we were able to get a hold of someone at any time. They explained everything thoroughly

and made sure that we understood everything that was happening. Moving is stressful enough, but having the wrong agent only amplifies the stress. The Oyler Group helps reduce the stress of moving by being completely transparent and honest at all times."

—Eric R.

"My wife and I worked with the Oyler Group for the sale of our home in Oakley. We have moved a number of times over the past 10 years, and have never experienced as much professionalism as we did with the Oyler Group. Everything (market overview, marketing plan, staging, pricing, negotiating the sale) was done with a level of knowledge, perspective and diligence that exceeded our expectations. We will be using the Oyler Group again in the future! Thanks Scott, Heather & Team!"

—Steve R.

"Scott, Heather & the entire Oyler Group team are the best in the business! They went above & beyond with each step of the selling process - everything felt very customized, personal & tailored to our specific needs. Their knowledge of the market is impeccable & I can't recommend them strongly enough for any future buyers or sellers!"

—Leif E.

"Scott and Heather seamlessly guided us through the daunting process of selling our first home. They provided expert advice regarding the timing of our listing, and listing price based on current inventory. We were provided a staging consultation and professional photography.

Scott gave us confidence throughout the negotiation process, and was always very responsive. Highly recommend!"

—Jason P. and Kendra K.

"The Oyler Group was fantastic. Scott was extremely personable and knowledgeable at our initial meeting, which is what triggered us to choose him as our agent (we interviewed 5 other agents). He really had great knowledge of the area and articulated and displayed his group's capabilities and previous successes. Thereafter, he and his team did a great job of helping us get our house ready for photos and listing. The whole process of getting listed took about 3-4 days. The photos were fantastic, the listing was well written and attractive, and the broad marketing was comforting in that we felt folks would see it. From the perspective of the showings, we downloaded an app that allowed us to approve or reject visits from other agents and their buyers. This was great because we could see everything in one place and could control the flow as needed (although we didn't reject any visits because we obviously wanted to sell). Once we had an offer, Scott was really helpful in negotiating and he made sure to maximize the sale price. He was confident in what we could realistically get for the home, and he was just about spot on. This was great because we ended up exceeding our initial expectations, but I feel it was reasonable and helpful for the neighborhood as well. Heather was also fantastic throughout the entire process. She was very responsive when we needed her, and was extremely proactive in helping walk us through the entire sales process, including closing. She also joined us at the closing and made sure everything was in good order. Overall, VERY happy with

Scott and his group and I'd highly recommend them to anyone looking to sell their home."

—Ana L.

"Scott and his team handled our home sale beautifully. He came into a listing presentation, told us what he was going to do and delivered as promised. Our showings went well. Communication was excellent and clear. Really nothing more could have been asked for."

—Michael M.

About Scott Oyler

Scott Oyler and his team help buyers and sellers with their real estate transactions in the greater Cincinnati, Ohio area that includes northern Kentucky. Affiliated with Coldwell Banker West Shell in Cincinnati, he has over 10 years of real estate sales experience and more than $300 million in successful transaction volume. Scott is licensed in Ohio and Kentucky.

Scott has consistently achieved a high level of sales performance and has won a number of awards for sales achievement, including:

- Nationally ranked at #88 in units sold in the "Real Trends 1000," compiled by "Real Trends" and the "Wall Street Journal," listing the top 1000 real estate professionals in America
- NRT National Leadership Award, #6 in Units Sold
- Cincinnati Area Board Of Realtors® (CABR) #3 Agent based on production
- Top 1% of Coldwell Banker Agents worldwide

Scott has also appeared on the Cincinnati Fox 19 Morning Show and HGTV's House Hunters as an expert on real estate trends in the area.

For more information about Scott Oyler, visit https://www.OylerGroup.com.

Buying and Selling Homes in Intown Atlanta Neighborhoods

Tonya Marlatt

Introduction

Tonya Marlatt specializes in the Intown Atlanta markets where she lives and has extensive experience helping buyers and sellers with their real estate transactions. Although she is geographically specific, she helps a wide range of clients from first-time home buyers to buyers and sellers of multimillion-dollar luxury homes. Real estate is in Tonya's blood as her parents always dabbled in real estate. She has a great passion for properties as she has moved 19 times within Intown Atlanta in the 25 years she has lived there.

Before becoming a licensed Georgia Real Estate Agent in 2002 and a licensed Real Estate Broker in 2006, Tonya worked for AT&T and helped the company launch wireless service in Atlanta and Charlotte.

In this chapter, Tonya provides insight for buyers and sellers in the Intown Atlanta markets. She discusses successfully securing a contract and then the process of getting from the contract to the closing.

Buying Your Home – Getting to the Contract

The first step in the home buying process is to identify monthly payments you can afford, or you are comfortable making. Remember to consider the impact of property taxes, insurance, and HOA (Homeowner's Association) fees if you are considering a condominium property. I don't recommend looking at homes until you have your budget clarified. It's easy to fall in love with a home that may not be affordable, and that ends up becoming the standard to judge all the other homes you view. It just makes the process a lot more challenging.

Talking with an experienced mortgage professional will help you understand the amount of loan for which you can be qualified along with the monthly payments at different loan amounts. It's not uncommon to discover that you can qualify for a larger loan than you had expected. This is another important reason to get your financing lined up at the beginning of the process. When you find your ideal home and want to make an offer, the seller and listing agent will expect you to present proof of pre-qualification from a lender along with the offer. Otherwise the seller may not even consider your offer. In a competitive market a buyer who has not been pre-qualified is at a distinct disadvantage. It is important to choose a lender and loan officer that takes the time upfront to determine your situation and properly assess your qualification. In some situations, a loan officer can do the underwriting upfront and provide a loan pre-approval based on more detailed financial information than provided during the application process. The lender relationship is critical to the success of a home purchase and an experienced real estate agent should be able to guide you through the process of selecting a reliable lender.

After establishing a budget, I suggest making a list of the things you need and want in your new home. The list would include things like number of bedrooms and bathrooms, size of home and lot, preferred neighborhood(s), school district, and other characteristics important to you. Communicating this information along with your budget to your agent helps narrow down areas and homes that will be of the most interest. The "wish list" is a starting point and you will probably find that your preferences are modified during the search.

Prices differ widely among Intown Atlanta neighborhoods, so your budget and requirements will dictate which specific neighborhoods will be a good match for you. Similar homes may vary in price by thousands of dollars between one neighborhood and another, only a short distance apart.

Often it becomes a balancing act between the budget, size of home, neighborhood, and your "wish list."

As an example, we have a very popular neighborhood called Inman Park where a three bedroom/two bathroom single-family home will be in the range of $650,000-$1,000,000+. If you go a just about a mile south into a neighborhood called Reynoldstown, you can buy a similar house for about $450,000. But there are people who specifically want to live in Inman Park. So, if their budget is only $450,000, then they will not be able to buy a three bedroom/two bathroom house in that neighborhood. There are options, however, to purchase a condo property around that price.

You can find most available properties online, but it's not always easy to identify homes that will meet your needs. As an agent, I believe there's a lot more to making a list of potentially suitable homes than just running a property report that, on the surface, lists houses that seem to meet your needs. It's important to go into the individual listings to see all the details which will narrow down a list that might be 60 homes long into a manageable list that better reflects what you are personally looking for based on your specific needs and wants. My experience shows that clients' preferences almost always change during the search. We want to avoid any missed opportunities, so initially the property lists may be relatively long. Let's say a client has expressed a preference for a kitchen with stained cabinets. While researching, I discover a home that appears to meet most of the initial requirements except the kitchen cabinets are white. Given it only differs in a minor way, I prefer to include such a house because time and again I have discovered that preferences change during the home search.

Market conditions change based on the supply and demand. We've experienced a period where the inventory of available homes has been at a relatively low level, making it harder to find a suitable property, especially in a specific neighborhood. This calls for a creative solution to find suitable homes that are not currently listed. Agents don't typically list properties until the homes are prepared for listing. When I have a client interested in a specific neighborhood and we can't find the right home, I reach out to my network of local agents that work in the area and describe what my client is looking for. Many times, I'll find a property match that isn't yet on the market. This has proven over-and-over to be a successful approach and often my client can purchase a property off-market. At a minimum, they are well positioned to put in an offer as soon as the listing goes active and ahead of other potential buyers. If the target is a specific condominium complex with no relevant listings, I have written letters to all the owners telling them I have a buyer for their unit. This is another proactive way to get an owner to sell a property that's not on the market.

You've found the home of your dreams, but how do you know the pricing reflects market value? I assist my clients with the value analysis. This is a similar process as that used to help a seller establish a listing price. There is a lot of science that goes into valuing a home. It's important to compare sales and metrics like square footage, the number of bedrooms/bathrooms, age, etc. All properties are different, so there is also an art involved. Identifying the different qualities of each home and how the unique attributes translate into value is critical. This takes a lot of experience and it helps when the agent has concentrated experience in a specific local area.

Crafting the right offer price is often the most significant factor when you have identified a home to purchase. When the market is tight and there is a lot of competition among buyers, other factors become important as well. Sellers are looking for offers that minimize the number and length of contract contingencies, like for inspections, appraisals, and financing approval. As discussed earlier, sellers and listing agents are looking for a strong indication of pre-qualification for mortgage financing and from a lender that has a reputation for being able to close on time. Sellers are also looking for clean, uncomplicated offers. Sellers are often anxious during the time between when they finalize a contract and the closing. It goes a long way if the seller initially feels like the buyer is well qualified and the contract is straightforward and without an excessive number of special stipulations.

Selling Your Home – Getting to the Contract

Real estate is a very geographically specific and working with an agent that has extensive local neighborhood experience can make the process and the outcome more favorable when selling a home. Agents that are not local experts tend to rely much more heavily on the science when valuing properties. That works in some markets, but it doesn't work well in our Intown market here in Atlanta. Understanding the art of valuing properties is just as important. For example, it's critical to understand that a beautifully decorated corner unit in a certain complex will bring another $50/square foot versus the one that's facing the railroad tracks. It's also important to understand changes on the horizon that could impact future values. Proximity to the developing Beltline or school zoning redistricting will probably impact value. There's a risk of underpricing properties without a good knowledge of the neighborhood and how the uniqueness of specific properties affects value.

When your home goes on the market, I want to make sure it is as attractive to potential buyers as possible. We also want to minimize distractions so that buyers can focus on the home itself. One of the most important steps is to neutralize the colors. If you have walls with bright colors, they should be painted in neutral tones. Buyers have a hard time envisioning themselves living in a home when there is loud paint they don't appreciate. They also don't want to have to paint as soon as they move in. Most people shopping for homes have watched shows on HGTV. Invariably there's a home that has a bright red wall that everyone on the show talks negatively about. You don't want that to be your house.

The nature of our Intown properties is that they tend to be smaller and the owners have accumulated a lot of stuff, so the homes can appear crowded. Another important preparation step is decluttering your home. An open, uncrowded home appears larger. Also, we don't want buyers distracted as they are walking through the home wondering where their belongings will go. As an example, let's say you have all your luggage stored in the corner of a room. There's a tendency for people walking through your home to look at the corner and think, "Oh, that's where the luggage goes." You'll be moving anyway, so pack up all the extra things you don't need and put them into a storage unit. I don't believe the home needs to be depersonalized, because people can see that someone lives in the home and they may make some connection with the family living there.

The home needs to be thoroughly cleaned and obvious repairs should be completed before we list. Even small things matter, like a light switch that's not working or a burned-out light bulb, because buyers will wonder what else is wrong. If the home has a yard, it should be free of debris and well-manicured.

As most people are looking at listings online, we need to make sure that the initial online impression is positive and makes the property stand out from all the others. Professional photography is a big part of making that great first impression. It's critical to capture the best and most compelling attributes of the home so it pops when buyers are searching through online postings. Technology is always changing, and drone videos are becoming more and more popular. There's a complex where I do a lot of listings and I had a drone video made that shows the entire complex and it's setting in the neighborhood. I use this in my listings so people can view the video online and get a full picture of the lifestyle and what it feels like to live there.

Written descriptions in listings are sometimes just an afterthought; however, I think the description is very important in explaining the features unique to the property, especially features that buyers can't see in the photos. If a condominium property has two parking spaces and the other units don't, that's an important point to call out.

Proximity to things like transit corridors, a walking path, a dog park, and other amenities are also important to describe.

When we list on the MLS (Multiple Listing Service), our listings are automatically syndicated to the most popular real estate websites, where consumers are looking for homes. Zillow is probably the most popular site. I have a premium membership that provides better placement of my listings, so people searching for a home can more easily find my listings.

One of my favorite strategies is pre-marketing the listing while the home is getting prepared, but before it is on the market. This works best when the inventory is low and when buyers are having difficulty finding what they are looking for. With pre-marketing I create excitement even before we list and show the home. I put out the word to my agent database about the upcoming listing as they often have an interested buyer and appreciate the opportunity to give their buyer a head start. I put the listing on Zillow as "Coming Soon" and if it's a single-family home, I'll put up a yard sign indicating "Coming Soon." This builds a database of interested buyers and buyer's agents I contact as soon as the listing goes active. Although we get requests for showings before the listing, my general policy is to hold off the showings until the listing date. This creates a lot of urgency among buyers and often leads to a quick sale.

Sellers should plan to be away from the home during showings and make arrangements for their pets to be removed from the property as well.

Technology is a big part of our everyday life and some homeowners have security video cameras installed outside and inside their home. This can raise privacy concerns, so I always recommend having a notice posted in the listing that video cameras are used inside the property.

From the Contract to Closing

You've gotten to the contract; what comes next? There are still several critical steps and some potential pitfalls in getting to the closing. Whether you are on the buying or selling end, an experienced agent can help reduce the stress during this important stage. The contract specifies an exact timeline for certain actions and removal of contingencies that must be strictly followed as you progress toward closing. During the Due Diligence Period, a buyer typically has the right to terminate for just about any reason. It's important for a seller to understand the contractual obligations. I help my clients understand the language in the contract documents and make sure they follow the timeline. Occasionally one party to a contract will not remember what was agreed. I've had a case where the seller was obligated to leave certain appliances in the home. Unfortunately, the seller sold the appliances to a third party and that created a last-minute frustration for all parties. It also ended up being a significant cost for the seller as he had to purchase new appliances to satisfy the contractual commitment and ensure the closing took place.

Getting to the closing can be very emotional for both parties and it's important to remember that the ultimate goal for everyone is to get to the closing table. A big part of an agent's job is to keep everyone calm. The agents on both sides should have a good, positive relationship and ensure there's a factual exchange of information and limit emotionally charged conversations. I remind my clients that I am there to represent their interest but it's also important to remember that there's another human being on the other side of the transaction.

Inspections are one of the hardest steps because the inspection findings often reopen negotiations regarding necessary repairs. The negotiations can become difficult and emotional because the buyers have already envisioned themselves living in the house and sellers are already thinking about packing and moving. If an inspection report comes back with a lot of findings, the seller thinks, "You'd guess my house wasn't even standing based on the way the inspector evaluated it." Buyers are likely to think, "Everything is wrong with this house." This period presents one of the greatest challenges to balance between the two sets of emotions and make progress toward closing. Even with minor findings, sometimes sellers don't want to repair something that may cost as little as $200 due to their emotions.

Buyers choose the inspectors and I have excellent inspectors I can recommend. It's important to identify an inspector who can convey the information without being overly alarmist. When I'm working with a buyer, I attend the wrap-up of the inspections, so the inspector can physically show me the findings that will be presented in a written report. This helps anticipate the potential issues and then I'm ready to advise the client on negotiation strategy. It is customary to communicate requested repairs in a contract amendment to address the concerns arising from the inspection.

As mentioned earlier, buyers will generally be pre-qualified before entering into a purchase contract, but issues can arise during the final underwriting. The pre-qualification reduces most of the risk, but job changes and other changes in a buyer's financial condition can sidetrack the process. Lenders also require that the appraisal comes in at or above the purchase price. This can be an issue when we are in a tight market and homes get bid up above the original listing price.

Closing disclosures are required to be presented three days before closing, so it's critical that these documents are presented on time to avoid delaying closing.

With the need to pay strict attention to all the due dates leading up to closing, I've deployed technology to keep my clients informed and to make the process more efficient. I use a software solution where I load a customized checklist based on fixed dates in the contract. The software sends out alerts before due dates, so all parties to the contract are on top of the schedule throughout the process.

Selecting the Best Agent for You

Buying or selling a home is a significant financial transaction, so I would recommend hiring someone who is an expert in their field. While most people want to hire the best accountant, financial advisor, or lawyer for advice, they often choose an acquaintance or relative to help them with a real estate purchase or sale, without considering their experience level. I suggest working with someone who is a full time, committed real estate professional. An agent who is experienced in the specific area where you are selling or intend to buy can make a large difference in the success of your transaction. Successfully completed transaction volume can be a good indicator of an agent's experience level. This information is generally available online. Testimonials and reviews are an indicator of how other clients view their satisfaction with the agent. You can also ask for references and talk directly with past clients.

You will have a short but intense working relationship with your agent, so it's important that you feel you can trust her to always work in your best interest and represent you as best as possible.

What Clients Are Saying

"You will not find a better Realtor® in Atlanta. Tonya made our first time home buying process such a great experience! She has tremendous knowledge of the market and has such a network in the area that she referred us to a group of people (lenders, inspectors, etc.) that we felt like we could truly trust.

"I highly recommend Tonya for any of your real estate needs!"

—Stacy P.

"I have bought/sold multiple homes in the past, and Tonya is the BEST agent I have worked with. I relied on her expertise on potential resell value and the area of town that is right for me. Most impressive is her network of contacts. Since I was relocating, I had a very tight window to schedule an inspection. She was able to contact an inspector over the weekend and have an inspection scheduled first thing on Monday. Tonya also remained attentive throughout the closing process to ensure a timely and smooth closing."

—Emi R.

"I had Tonya as my agent in an all cash sale with a professional musician who was on tour and very difficult to get in contact with. From the start when I first saw the property to the finish at closing only seven days later, Tonya was phenomenal. Ultra-responsive and extremely detail oriented, she made the process smooth. If you're looking for an aggressive agent who responds to any inquiry at any time of day within a minute, Tonya is the choice for you. I can't recommend her highly enough."

—Alan P.

"My fiancé and I loved working with Tonya for our first home purchase! She guided us through the process with ease and communicated both promptly and effectively. Not only is she an expert in her field, Tonya is highly approachable and made us feel comfortable asking lots of questions. What really sets Tonya far above the rest is her love for what she does; Her excitement and enthusiasm are palpable! She is our forever agent and there is no one we trust more with our future real estate needs."

—Amanda P.

"Tonya is very knowledgeable about the market and this was especially helpful with the appraisal. The buyer's agent pointed to the selling price on the last sale of a 2-bedroom unit as a comparable. But that had been almost two years ago. Tonya was able to point out recent comparable sales in neighboring building that demonstrated how values had gone up significantly since that last sale in our building."

—Daniel H.

"I have worked with Tonya on many real estate transactions over the years. She is absolutely the smartest person I have met in real estate -and I have met many. She fully understands all Atlanta neighborhoods and can guide you to the area that best meets your needs. She is brilliant when it comes to contract negotiation. She makes sure your needs are met while making sure the folks on the other side of the transaction are treated fairly. Her knowledge of the real estate market in general as well as her understanding of the Atlanta neighborhood's nuances makes her your best resource when buying or selling real estate in Atlanta! I cannot recommend her highly enough!"

—Mellisa H.

About Tonya Marlatt

Tonya Marlatt is a transplant from Michigan and after 25 years, proudly calls Atlanta home. She is a licensed Georgia Real Estate Broker in Atlanta where she helps buyers and sellers in all price ranges. Tonya focuses in the Intown Atlanta neighborhoods where she lives and has extensive local knowledge. She has been representing buyers and seller since 2002.

Tonya is committed to making her clients' real estate transactions an easy and enjoyable experience. She is passionate about real estate and loves the feeling of walking out of a closing knowing she helped write the first sentence in the next chapter of her client's life story.

For more information about Tonya Marlatt, visit http://www.TonyaMarlatt.com.

Building a Real Estate Team to Make Your Transaction as Smooth and Easy as Possible

Jon Holsten

Introduction

Jon Holsten is an award-winning Broker Associate affiliated with Windermere Real Estate in Fort Collins, Colorado. Jon helps buyers and sellers with their real estate transactions in Fort Collins and throughout the surrounding Northern Colorado area.

After graduating from Colorado State University, Jon started his professional career in journalism. From journalism he went into law enforcement, serving on the Fort Collins Police Department for 17 years where he honed his communication, negotiation, and leadership skills.

In this chapter, Jon describes his philosophy of making home buying or selling an enjoyable experience for clients using teamwork approach based on trust.

Building a Transaction Team Based on Trust

My business model is very simple and can be shared in a few seconds. My goal is to help someone buy or sell their home at the right time, to or from the right person, for the right price, and then to have them look back on the experience and say it was about as easy as it could have been.

The typical perception is that a real estate transaction is very complicated, will likely be a negative experience, and potentially very frustrating or stressful, but if you have the right people involved, it should be a pretty simple process. Can a real estate transaction be enjoyable? Absolutely. There are certain things in the process that you can't control, but there are many aspects that can be. It comes down to the correct strategy and choosing the right agent and supporting team to help you through the process.

While most people believe it's just them and their real estate agent who are involved in a transaction, the reality is – it takes a team effort. In addition to the buyer or seller, the team will likely include a lender, inspectors, the title company, as well as other professionals, depending on the situation. The buyers or sellers on the other side of the transaction and their agent are also involved in the process. I view my responsibility as a real estate agent to bring in a team perspective and to run interference for my clients, whether buyers or sellers, and to make the overall process very positive.

If you are travelling down the road and don't know where you are headed, it will be frustrating for everyone. Communication is an essential element of making sure you and your agent are on the same page and both understand your goals and objectives in buying or selling a home. You should expect your agent to take the time to clearly understand your specific needs, concerns and what you are ultimately trying to achieve. It can be an emotional experience and you should get a sense that your agent truly cares about your situation and will have the patience to help you navigate through the entire process, keeping you informed, and answering any questions that you have.

Buying or selling a home is a very interactive process and timely communication is critical to success. One of the biggest complaints about working with a real estate agent is a lack of communication. A real estate agent who doesn't communicate with their client is simply not doing his or her job. There are many ways for buyers and sellers to stay connected with their agent through the process. Some people prefer phone calls, others like to communicate by text message or email. In rare occasions, a carrier pigeon may come in to play. Ok, just kidding about the carrier pigeon!

It is important to have communication with your agent to a degree that you feel cared for. Some buyers and sellers want to hear from their agent every day. Weekly may be enough for others, and some don't want to be bothered unless there is a problem with the transaction. One of the very first things I do when I'm working with a new client is to make sure I understand how (and how much) they like to communicate, and then be committed to making that happen.

As you are selecting an agent, make sure all of your initial questions are answered and that they offer information and/or advice that you didn't even think about. Also, pay attention to that initial indication as to whether you will enjoy being around the agent and interacting with them regularly. If not, that's a red flag. Buying or selling a home is a very significant event in your life on many levels, to include emotional and financial. You've got to feel comfortable that your agent is trustworthy and looking out for your needs. Your choice of real estate agent is critical to your transaction success.

When you interview agents, ask about how they will handle the process. If you are selling your home, inquire about how they will be marketing your home and if they have the budget to spend on advertising and other important resources. It needs to be a team effort, so who do they have to recommend for other members of your real estate team?

If you don't already have an established relationship with an agent, consider asking friends or relatives for recommendations of agents who they've had a positive experience with. You can also do some research online. Look at reviews to see what clients are saying. You can generally find information online indicating an agent's success in the community and their overall reputation. Choose wisely.

Buying Your Home

Defining Goals and Objectives

Most people have a general understanding of what they're looking for when they are considering buying a home. They may not have written down a list of their needs and wants, but they likely have a mental picture of their wants and needs. Occasionally I meet with homebuyers who have a hard time defining what their ideal home looks like. Put some time into figuring out exactly what you need before you spend much time on your search. It is not just about the house itself. Think about your family's needs, lifestyle, and what things will make your life more enjoyable. The right school zone is likely important for families with children. What conveniences and amenities are you looking for? Proximity to shopping, entertainment, and recreational opportunities are important for most people, as well.

I consider it one of my responsibilities to help clients narrow their search. For couples, I'll ask them to individually write down a list of the top five things they are looking for in a new home, hoping that key preferences float to the top of that list. Sometimes the lists diverge from each other, which makes the process a little more challenging.

Several years ago, I was working with a couple moving into the community from out of state. Their preferences were about as opposite as you can imagine! We looked at several homes. The wife wanted to live on the water, while the husband didn't want to look at a lake. The husband wanted a two-car garage; the wife said less than a three-car garage was unacceptable. There were several other preferences that were not aligned. To make progress, I changed the exercise to listing the top three things each could *not* live without, instead of what they were looking for. This helped the couple realize where their primary goals overlapped and narrowed down the search parameters. Interestingly, they made an offer on the first home we visited after that exercise. I've used that tactic several times now, and it works! It can also reduce the number of homes you'll look at, and the time it takes to find the right one.

Working with a Lender

Buyers who need financing to purchase their new home should start working with a lender right off the bat. Many buyers start their search, only to find out well down the road that they have been looking at homes they can't afford, or perhaps not looking at homes that are easily affordable for them. Worst case scenario is finding out they don't even qualify for a loan. This is both frustrating and disappointing for the buyer. Competent real estate agents will insist that potential buyers jump on this task right away to avoid a wild goose chase.

A lender will help walk you through the process of determining how much of a home you can afford and what your monthly payments will look like. When you find the right home, the seller will likely require a letter from a lender confirming you qualify for the loan to purchase. If you don't already have that letter in hand, you could easily miss out on your dream home because someone else was prepared, and you were not.

Many buyers will qualify for a loan they simply can't afford. Sometimes the best approach is to determine the maximum monthly payment you are comfortable making and have the lender reverse engineer the payment amount back to the price point that fits with that payment. If you don't immediately qualify for a mortgage, or you can't quite hit the value of homes that fit your needs, a good lender will show you the path to getting your finances in order, which may include paying off consumer debt, or perhaps credit score repair.

It's also important to understand other constraints. Let's say you recently started a successful business and are excited to buy a new home. Although you have a good income, when you speak with a lender, you may find that you need to wait until you have at least two years of successful self-employment in order to qualify for a loan. Some lenders aren't as confident in your business as you may be! It's better to get this knowledge upfront rather than spending a lot of time looking at homes that you can't buy.

Your lender is key member of your transaction team and just as it is with your real estate agent, choosing the right lender is critical. Some people pick a lender based on cost. Of course, you need to look at your out-of-pocket cost, but sometimes it's worth paying a little more to work with a reputable lender, than to spend less money on fees and have a miserable experience. I've seen a $500 swing in that number make for a miserable or positive experience. By the way, there can be hidden fees in loans that make one lender look better than another, when in fact it may not be the case.

Look for a lender that has a great track record and reputation. Oftentimes, working with a lender in your community is best, simply because they know local market challenges and are known to local agents. This can make a difference when your offer is reviewed by a seller and their agent has had a positive experience with that specific lender. It can work the other way, as well. So, again ... choose your lender wisely.

Your agent should have a list of solid, reputable lenders they can recommend. Make sure they provide you with several names so you can interview them and make sure it's a good fit.

<u>Making an Offer</u>

When you find the right home, and you're ready to submit an offer, your agent will help you with all necessary documents that need to be completed.

There are some decisions to be made at this point. You need to settle on a price you're willing to pay for the home. If you have questions about the true value of a home in relation to what a seller is asking for, have your agent run a search for comparable properties that have sold in the recent past.

There is a delicate balance between making a "good value" offer and potentially insulting a seller with a low-ball number they can't swallow. I recommend to my buyers that if they feel the asking price is reasonable and the home is "the one" for them, they get as close to the asking price as they feel comfortable. If it is clearly overpriced, your offer should be accompanied by an explanation from your agent as to how you came to that conclusion.

While the price offered for a home is often seen as the most important element, it may not be for the seller. Sometimes, they may be more interested in the type of loan you're using, closing timeline and other terms. The highest offer is not always the best offer.

When the market is weaker and fewer buyers are looking for homes, there is more room to negotiate the price. In a hot market, when the price has been bid up, there is a concern that although the price seems fair, the appraisal will not come in at a level that will justify the agreed upon purchase price. This is a complex situation and can affect the financing approval, so you and your agent need to exercise caution when making an offer that may be over the anticipated appraised value.

Except for in special cases, an inspection contingency is included in the contract. That clause generally allows the buyer to walk away from the deal if the inspection findings are not suitable. Or, in some states, sellers are required to address certain deficiencies, like electrical and plumbing problems. If you are aware of potential deal breakers before you put in the offer, I recommend addressing those issues in the original offer.

Timing can also be an important factor for both the buyer and seller. Some considerations include the timeline for inspections and other contingencies, like financing approval and the appraisal. Some sellers may wish to remain living in the home for a period of time after closing. When the buyer is agreeable, that can really be attractive to the seller. Important timing issues need to be communicated in the offer and may be negotiated in the process of reaching a signed agreement.

Contract to Closing

Most re-sale home purchase contracts are state approved and extremely buyer-friendly. They allow for several contingencies like the inspection I mentioned, as well as title work, appraisal, financing, and home owner association documents acceptance (if applicable). These generally give the buyer the ability to exit the contract legally and retain their earnest money (basically a deposit) that they typically put down when the contract is signed. The timeline for removing contingencies is specifically defined and should be understood and followed. It's critical to understand what you are agreeing to when you sign a contract and your commitment to meet the described timeline. Your agent should take the time to go through the contract with you, so you understand all the terms and conditions and what you are agreeing to.

Sometimes getting under contract can be the easiest part of a transaction because there's still a lot more that needs to happen. Only so much can be controlled by the buyer or seller, and what can be controlled needs to be diligently addressed. There are deals that go through with no issues at all, but there are usually some curveballs thrown at all parties. Some transactions will hit roadblock after roadblock, so it's a matter of getting through them unscathed. Your agent should be able to communicate well with the other side, so the hurdles can be overcome. At the end of the day, the seller wants to sell, and the buyer wants to buy. It's a matter of getting the job done in a way that's acceptable for everyone involved.

Selling Your Home

<u>Objectives for the Sale</u>

The first step in selling your home is to define your objectives and understand the timeline for selling. Many homeowners are intimidated by the selling process and don't have a good understanding of all that is involved in selling their home. An initial conversation with an experienced real estate agent can help clarify the steps that are required in selling and the anticipated timeline from listing to closing. You will need to sign a contract with your agent detailing the responsibilities of all parties, as well as real estate fees to be charged. Your agent should thoroughly review with you any agreement you are signing so that everyone has a clear understanding of the terms.

Some important things to consider and discuss, so you have a clear picture of where you are headed:

- Where are you moving to?
- Are you already in the process of buying a new home or do you already have a new home that you are moving to?
- Do you need to get the cash out of your existing home to buy a new home?
- If you are moving to a different area, is there a time schedule for when you need to be in the new location?

Pricing Your Home for the Market

Pricing is often the major component to selling your home in a reasonable amount of time. Sellers set the asking price, but the market determines the value, so it's critical to get an expert evaluation of your home's market value. Most people interested in selling their home have an idea of what their home is worth and have looked at some of the online real estate sites that show estimates of value. Don't rely on these online estimated values as they are based on general statistics and the computer algorithms they use don't have any information on condition or level of improvements and finishes in your home, or any other home for that matter. These computer estimates are more often wrong than they are right, and they may over or under value your home.

It is important to have someone with market experience to review your specific home and neighborhood to give you a more accurate value or to at least confirm the numbers. I always complete a comparative market analysis for my clients, comparing their home to other recent sales of the most similar homes in their neighborhood and surrounding area. Factors we consider include square footage, lot size, numbers of bedrooms and bathrooms, overall condition, style, level of improvements and finishes, location, amenities, and other details.

Most homeowners have great pride of ownership, which is great. Oftentimes, however, they will tend to assign more value to their home than the market will support. Maybe they have made substantial improvements and expect that the home value was increased by the amount spent. For example, $50,000 was put into a basement finish and the expectation is that the improvement increased the value by $50,000. Unfortunately, it typically doesn't work that way and it's difficult to get the full amount spent on improvements.

When your home is listed it's critical to closely align the list price to the market value. There is a common misconception that if you set the price higher than what you are expecting, there is room to negotiate and that you can always drop the price. The reality is that buyers are usually looking for home in a specific price range and if your home is over-priced, they may not even consider it, because it's outside of their range. Even if buyers do look at an over-priced home, they may realize it's not priced correctly based on other homes they have seen.

Your best shot at selling is right after the home has gone on the market. This is because serious buyers and their agents are closely watching for new listings, and possibly getting new listing alerts emailed to them. If your home lingers on the market and you reduce the price later, you've already missed all those buyers, and it's tough to get them back. Another concern is that buyers wonder what is wrong with a home that has sat on the market for a longer than normal period, and they just see this as an opportunity for a low-ball offer. Price your home right the first time!

<u>Preparing Your Home for Sale</u>

When your home is on the market, a great presentation to lookers is critical. Just as you detail a car when selling, you need to detail your home before the first person sees it. I provide a stager for my sellers to make sure everything possible is done to make the home attractive from the get-go.

Some homeowners have it in their mind that they need to make major improvements before selling, like update a kitchen, finish the basement, or redo the landscaping. It's true that such improvement may help you sell faster, but as I mentioned earlier, it's rare to get your money back out of the improvement, and that's why I encourage a very cautious approach when considering improvement projects prior to selling. Sometimes major changes can make sense, but more often not. If your budget is limited, I suggest focusing on minor changes that are more likely to help the home show well, and have a good chance of returning most if not all of your investment. These projects often include painting, cleaning, or replacing flooring. You'll also want to invest time, energy, and money into addressing some other smaller cosmetic items.

The buyer will typically have the home inspected after the purchase contract is signed. If the home inspector finds issues needing repair, you can expect the buyer to request those repairs be made, or they may ask you to credit them the cost of those repairs. If major problems are discovered during the inspection, the buyer may choose to terminate the deal and retain their earnest money if the contract allows. For this reason, I often suggest sellers have their home pre-inspected so there are no major surprises.

Before listing, the home needs to be thoroughly cleaned, and the landscaping well-manicured. Think about the pathway from where potential buyers will park and then walk up to your front door. Make sure everything on that path and the front entrance to your home appears to be in very good condition, as this is where they are getting their first impression.

Pets are an important and sensitive subject. Sometimes pets have caused damage and any evidence of pet damage needs to be addressed. Most homeowners have become used to pet smells in their home, but visitors, some of whom may have allergies, are generally going to pick up on pet odors. This can be a little humbling to deal with, but if you want to achieve the best results, pet odors need to be eliminated.

The final stage in home preparation is to make it appear open, bright and uncluttered. You want potential buyers to imagine how their possessions will fit in the home. You'll be moving soon anyway, so pack up the things you won't be using and remove them from the home. A staging consultant may recommend removing some pieces of furniture as well to open up the home. Consider utilizing a nearby storage unit to minimize your home's contents. A well-staged home frequently wins out over one that's not staged and may well result in a higher purchase price.

Marketing and Exposure

When your home is clean, staged, and decluttered, it's time for a photo shoot. Your photos will be used in online listings, social media, and possibly brochures. Quality photography is essential to make the very best first impression when buyers are searching online, so I always use a professional photographer, experienced in capturing the beauty and elegance of the home. You should insist on this with your real estate agent. I carefully select the best shots to use for the online listing and put those photos in the order which best show features of the home. Again, this is the first impression for most buyers.

It is super important to take advantage of today's popular technology platforms to expose your home to the most buyers. We want to be where the buyers are, so social media is becoming more important, especially Facebook, YouTube, and Instagram.

Your neighbors can be a good a source of promoting your home. They may have friends or relatives that may be interested in moving to the neighborhood, so we like to alert them to the listing. I recommend sending out "Just Listed" postcards to the neighborhood to make sure everyone knows about it – and has the information to pass along. Open houses can create additional interest. There's a lot of debate on how well open houses work in marketing a home, but frequently neighbors come for a look, so it's another opportunity for exposure to a group of people who can direct a buyer your way.

An agent's marketing and promotional efforts are designed to get buyers into your home for a look. Showings may be a hassle, but they're critical to getting your home sold. I would encourage you to be as flexible as possible to accommodate showings, even with little notice, because you generally only have one shot at a buyer. They may be visiting from out of the area and may have a limited schedule, or they may make an offer on another home if they can't see yours.

Keep your home clean and show ready during the time it is listed. You have to live your life, but it does take a daily effort to keep everything neat and tidy around the home. Pets should not be around the home during showings, so put together a strategy to be able to take them with you during showings. Boarding may be an option during the daytime hours.

Reviewing Offers

The goal, of course, is to get an offer in hand as soon as possible. When reviewing offers with your agent, it's important to consider the net price after any concessions that may be requested. As I mentioned earlier, if you're fortunate enough to have multiple offers, the contract with the highest price is not always the best offer. There are several variables to consider. Most purchases are going to be funded with a mortgage, and as I recommend buyers to obtain a letter from a lender which shows they're pre-qualified for a loan, I always encourage my sellers to require that same letter be included with an offer.

An all cash offer can be very strong if backed up with proof of funds to close, which I recommend sellers require just like a lender letter. An offer that waives an appraisal contingency, meaning the buyer puts additional cash into the purchase if the appraisal doesn't substantiate the purchase price, can be attractive and reduces some seller risk. Is the buyer requesting other contingencies? A buyer that needs to sell an existing home to close on purchasing your home adds additional complications and risk to a deal.

It is not necessarily a simple process comparing different offers to understand the pros and cons of each, along with risk factors that may make some offers less attractive than others. Experienced, competent representation can help you assess one or more offers and help guide you to a decision.

What you want to avoid is getting into a contract, in essence taking the home off the market, and then not getting to the closing table with a buyer.

Contract to Close

I discussed earlier the pathway from an accepted purchase contract to the closing from the buyer's perspective. The same concepts apply for the seller. The usual contingencies to get past are the inspection, title work, financing, and the appraisal. A contract typically allows the buyer to step out of the contract at several stages along the way. The seller, however, is generally locked in once they sign the contract. As a seller, make sure you are very comfortable with all terms before you sign on the line.

Buying or selling a home should overall be a smooth process. Again, issues will surface along the way, but a competent and communicative agent will help you maintain the right perspective and keep the task on track.

What Clients Are Saying

"Jon was an incredible resource and brought a tremendous amount of value to our home purchase. He was always at least one step ahead in the process and always kept us informed."

—Jeremy and Kathryn

"We can't imagine not working with someone who had our complete trust on such an important process. Jon was amazing and made the process as easy as possible."

—Dawnson and Sarah

"Jon was wonderful to work with, very friendly, professional, available and knowledgeable about properties and locations. It was so wonderful to have someone walk through the home buying process and feel like they really cared about you as a person and not just another home buyer."

—Nicholas & Sherry M.

"Jon is a great realtor who is very committed to his client's satisfaction. He is attentive unassuming and honest. The relationship we were able develop will last after this transaction is complete."

—Jason & Justin G.

"Working with Jon was a great experience. His process is well thought out and expertly executed. Two of the things I appreciated the most were his insight and tempered approach. Our property was under contract in 6 days and at full asking price. This clearly demonstrates property and comparative sales knowledge. We highly recommend Jon and his team!"

—Cash & Allison

"I just can't say enough about Jon. He was unbelievably helpful in a competitive market. He was always available, knowledgeable and creative with the contracts, honest and open about what the market conditions were really like when we were looking, and we felt like he was really on our side. Over a year after our home was purchased, he still checks in to see if everything is going well."

—John F.

About Jon Holsten

Jon Holsten grew up in Northern Colorado and graduated from Colorado State University. He has lived in Northern Colorado for over 25 years. Following careers in journalism and law enforcement, Jon became a real estate agent in 2012 and rapidly established himself as a respected authority in Northern Colorado residential sales.

Jon is affiliated with Windermere Real Estate and helps buyers and sellers in Fort Collins and the surrounding Northern Colorado area. He is a member of the National

Association of Realtors®, Colorado Association of Realtors®, and Fort Collins Board of Realtors®. Jon has been recognized by REAL Trends as one of America's Best Real Estate Agents, and the Wall Street Journal has identified Jon as one of America's top 1,000 Realtors®. He is nationally recognized as a high-volume producer by Ninja Selling.

For more information about Jon Holsten, visit www. HolstenRealEstate.com.

Selling Your St. Paul Area Home for the Highest Value

Kim Ziton

Introduction

Kim Ziton is affiliated with Keller Williams Premier Realty's Luxury Homes Division in Woodbury, Minnesota. She consistently has been one of the firm's top producers and is considered one of the top 20 agents worldwide among Keller Williams Premier Realty's over 139,000 agents. She has been the #1 Real Estate Agent in Minnesota from 2012-2018.

Kim helps clients with their real estate transactions in and around Woodbury in the eastern suburbs of St. Paul. With 27 years of real estate sales experience, Kim has been recognized for a number of awards for sales achievement including having been included in Real Trends America's Best Real Estate Agent list, which ranks agent sales volume in all 50 states.

With a passion for home design and decorating from an early age, Kim began her real estate career at Bearpath

Golf and Country Club in Eden Prairie, an 18-hole championship golf course designed by Jack Nicklaus. It is the only gated community in Minnesota. Her work representing custom builders gave her a strong education in home construction and custom design features. Kim was a new home consultant for Kootenia Homes, a custom home builder with multiple awards to their portfolio, such as the prestigious Reggie, Trillium and HAP awards. Kim represented Kootenia for over fifteen years selling homes and properties and in her last year for Michael Lee Inc., a division of Kootenia Homes.

Kim has successfully branded herself as an individual with tenacity and unquestionable market knowledge. With a keen eye for detail she provides intuitive and informed guidance in helping buyers find their dream home and achieving maximum value for the sale of a home. Given her previous role, Kim has gained a unique level of experience understanding the evolution and complexity of a home in new construction. Her clients have come to depend on her ability to quickly assess their needs and preferences while respecting their time and finances. She has a track record of success dealing with complex transactions, marketing strategy, and structure of a sale. Recognized for her efficiency and unique ability to connect with clients, Kim is well known for meeting and exceeding their goals aggressively but with finesse, from years of successful skilled negotiating experience.

She is well-respected in the real estate community, has built a reputation as hardworking, and being upfront and honest with every one of her clients. Kim's motto, "meet and exceed clients' goals." She is very hands-on. Her success has not made her unreachable, she is totally accessible, as her clients receive the highest level of personalized attention.

Kim holds her Real Estate License in both Minnesota and Wisconsin.

In this chapter Kim provides insights for home sellers in the greater St. Paul area that are interested in getting the most value from the sale of their homes.

Preparation is a Major Key to Selling for the Highest Price

Regardless of the market situation, we always have competition when we are selling a home. It may be new construction or existing resale homes. It's sort of a beauty contest and we only have one chance to make a good first impression on potential buyers. Even if it's a home that's not new, we need to present it in the best possible condition to sell for the highest price in the shortest amount of time. We want to make the home as much as possible look like a model house in a new development. It needs to be decluttered and depersonalized, so people looking at the home can visualize it as their own. Even though the home is furnished, thinking in terms of a model home, it should almost look as if no one is living there. Staging the home so it looks open, spacious, and inviting is also a critical part of preparation.

Buyers expect a home to be clean, well maintained, and with everything in good working condition. A meticulously maintained home demonstrates pride of ownership, which buyers appreciate. They don't want to purchase a home and immediately have to spend money on fixing things that need repair. Instead, they may want to make the home their own, investing in fun items like new countertops, a tile backsplash, or other custom features they prefer.

We generally think of making the first impression as people are walking into your home for the first time. This is true, but with most buyers starting their home search on the Internet, we have to think about making that great first impression online as well. We can achieve this with high quality pictures for the interior/exterior, aerial photos and Matterport tours that present the home at its best. Photos need to be shot after all of the preparations, including decluttering and staging, are completed.

Homes sell in this area all 12 months of the year, but the busiest time is from February through May. Activity slows down in the summer as people are traveling and on vacation and then picks up again in the fall, before slowing significantly over the holidays. If you have the opportunity to plan ahead for your home sale, you can organize the preparation over a few months to make sure everything is in order as the home is getting ready to be listed. This is especially important for the yard and exterior of the home that can't be worked on during the wintertime. Preparing the outside in spring or summer and getting good pictures at that time will help in selling the home even in the winter when we have snow on the ground.

Preparing your home to look its best does take time and energy, but doesn't necessarily have to cost a lot of money unless major repairs are required. A clean, well-maintained home will sell faster and for a higher price.

Systems and General Condition

Buyers are expecting that the major systems and structure of a home are in good in condition and they will be having inspections performed after the contract is signed. As a seller, it's better to know in advance that everything is in order. The furnace and air conditioning systems should be serviced if they have not been recently checked. An update report from an HVAC service company can indicate that the systems have been maintained. Have an electrician fix any electrical problems that you are aware of. You might not normally look under the sinks, but this is the time to check for any leaks and have a plumber make any necessary repairs. Clean the furnace and water heater and replace furnace filters if needed. Buyers will be looking at these small details that indicate a well cared for home.

Check the hardware on all doors, windows, and cabinets. Fix or replace any hardware that is not working properly. At the same time check for sticking and squeaks and remedy, as necessary. Look around the home for dings or scratches in the walls or baseboards. Repair and touch up the paint or apply a fresh coat of paint to the room. When re-painting, use a neutral paint tone, which will brighten up the space.

Of course, everything needs to be clean and free of odors. Clean the carpet, draperies, and furniture. Clean out the fireplace and if there are any smoke stains on the wall or mantle, they need to be removed. Replace burned out light bulbs.

Curb Appeal and Exterior

Imagine potential buyers driving up to your home and parking for a showing. As they are walking from the car to the front door, they have a few seconds to observe the front yard and entrance to the home. Those critical few seconds are when they are making their first impressions of your home and that influence their impression as they are walking through the inside as well. We only have one time to make a good first impression. In fact, the curb appeal is so important that some potential buyers may not even want to continue to see inside the home if the exterior doesn't show well.

First, walk out to the street and take a critical look at the yard and the front of the home. Imagine a buyer's first view of your property and what they will see. Does everything look like's it's in good shape or is there some need of repairs or cleaning?

Make sure the landscaping is well manicured. The lawn should be cut and edged along the walk and driveway. Weeds should be eliminated as much as possible in the lawn and planting areas. Remove any dead branches from trees as well as dead or dying shrubs. Trim the shrubbery and try to introduce some color with flowering plants, depending on the season.

Special attention needs to be given the front entryway. Buyers will stop here for a few seconds as they are waiting for the door to be opened and they are sure to be looking carefully at this area. A coat of paint on the front door, window trim, porch, and pillars will make everything look fresh. Make sure to keep this area very clean including removal of any cobwebs. Dress up the front door with a wreath or a new door hardware. The addition of some potted plants at the entry will make it more welcoming and add color.

Even small things matter. Make sure that the house numbers and mailbox are in good condition. Exterior lighting should be working, and any bad bulbs replaced. It's not uncommon for potential buyers to drive by your home in the evening, so keeping the exterior lights on in the evening will make your home look nice. Clean outdoor furniture thoroughly and organize it on the patio or deck.

All windows and screens should be cleaned. You should also walk around the house to see if there is any caulking that needs to be replaced. At the same time check to see if any of the exterior paint needs to be touched up. Are the roof, gutters and downspouts in good condition? Make sure the gutters are cleaned. If there are stains on the walk, driveway, or patio, pressure washing is recommended.

In the wintertime it can be quite difficult to get the yard and exterior ready. Even if you are not ready to list your home in the autumn, if you are able to plan ahead and get the work completed by the end of summer, we can come in and get the exterior pictures in August or September, when the leaves are still on the trees, the grass is green, and the flowers are in bloom. In this way you can be working toward getting the home ready for listing and we will still be able to display beautiful outside photos even in the winter or early spring.

Decluttering and Staging

Most individuals and families accumulate a lot of things over the years that are on display in their home. Your possessions make your home comfortable for you, but can overwhelm buyers looking at your home. As mentioned earlier, we want to make the home look as much as possible like a model home. This means it should appear open, light, spacious, and uncluttered. We want to maximize the potential for buyers to imagine themselves living in the home and this is difficult if the home is crowded with personal items, pictures, and artwork. We want buyers to focus on the home, itself, and not get distracted by all of your nice personal effects.

Buyers walking through the home are likely to look in closets and built-in cabinets throughout the house to see if space is available for their things. If these areas are packed, the impression is that there is not enough space. Imagine their reaction if they open a kitchen cabinet and it's so packed that something falls out. Remove most of the items on shelving and countertops as well to open up the space. You will be packing and moving, so pack up the things that you don't need while the home is listed to create openness through the home.

Along with minimizing clutter, we need to think about the flow through the home and the arrangement of furniture to make the home appear open, easy to walk through, and inviting. As an example, we may walk into a room and the couch is positioned so the back is facing us and it feels like we have to walk around it. We will move around the furniture and possibly remove a chair or two to open it up.

Many homes have smaller bedrooms for children and the furniture sometimes crowds the room. They may have a queen bed and three or four other pieces of furniture in the room. In this case we would remove some of the items, leaving the bed, one nightstand, and maybe a dresser or a desk. This will make the bedroom appear larger.

With staging, we present the home so each room has its own story or vignette; enough so it warms it up and gives the room some life, but not so much where people are distracted. We may arrange a tray with a book on it, or a couple of decorative pillows for a pop of color. Fresh flower arrangements and a little current artwork will also warm up the home. These little enhancements will increase attractiveness, not only when buyers are walking through the home, but also for the photos we will be using online and in other marketing materials.

Kitchens & Bathrooms

The kitchen is the most important room when buyers are looking at your home. When we look at online click-through rates of the pictures, the kitchen photos will always be viewed, and we can tell that people go back and look at them several times. Buyers walking through your home will also focus a lot of their attention on the kitchen. The kitchen is the best place to invest with updates and improvements to get most of your money back.

Styles and preferences change over time so it's best to get some professional advice before investing in improvements to make sure they are in line with current buyer expectations. White cabinets and stainless steel appliances are popular now. Cabinets can be painted white or the doors can usually be resurfaced. Many times, just switching out the hardware will update the look. Changing the countertops or backsplash may also improve the appearance if they are outdated. It may not take a lot of changes to transform the kitchen into a true gourmet kitchen.

All of the appliances should be in good working order and any damaged appliance knobs need to be replaced. Check for faucet leaks or drips and fix as necessary. This applies to the kitchen as well as the bathrooms.

Buyers are going to focus on the countertop and cabinet space, so don't leave them cluttered. Put away or pack away the majority of countertop appliances, canisters, or decorations on the kitchen counters. This will reinforce the appearance that there is adequate space. I suggest displaying a cookbook, possibly a little vignette, or a couple of cups and saucers for coffee or tea, and let everything else shine on its own, so there's nothing that's distracting. Look at the cabinet contents as well and remove some of the items to make it look like there is still space available. Items stored or displayed above the kitchen cabinets should be removed, as they can be a distraction while trying to appreciate the features of the kitchen.

Cleanliness is critical in the kitchen and bathrooms. Sinks, tubs, showers, and countertops should sparkle. Mirrors, glass, chrome and porcelain surfaces should be thoroughly cleaned. Grout for ceramic tile needs to be scrubbed, or stained if the grout cannot be completely cleaned. Replace failing caulking where necessary around tubs and showers. Replace any caulking with mold or mildew.

Small improvements, like updating a faucet and lighting or adding a custom framed mirror can refresh a bathroom. Of course, a fresh coat of paint can go a long way to create a fresh look. Remove soap dispensers and personal items. Make sure to hang new, fresh, clean towels and replace shower curtains and bathroom rugs with something fresh and tasteful. You also might consider adding a small orchid or other plant in the bathrooms.

Closets

Closets are always important to buyers because it seems like there is never enough closet space and we want to dispel that idea in their minds. First, pack away clothes and shoes that are not going to be used for the next few months and store in boxes neatly in the basement. If you don't have a basement or there is not enough space, storage space can be rented at a storage facility. Make sure there is empty space left in the closet and organize everything left very neatly on the bars and racks. Make sure the doors and drawers open and close easily and that the tracks are clean and clear. Eliminate any squeaking.

Garage

The garage is important for most buyers, because they want to know that their cars and other belonging will fit. Decluttering the garage is as important as the rest of the house so that people can see that there is enough space available. If you have stuff that you are not likely to ever use, now is the time to get rid of it. You can also rent a storage unit and take everything there that is not needed during the time the home is for sale. Organize your tools and other items left in the garage in an orderly manner. Buyers understand that you will be moving so it's okay to some extent to have organized stacks of boxes on one side of the garage, if necessary.

Clean the walls, shelves, floor, garage doors and windows. Repaint if necessary, especially if there are dings and scratches on the walls. Most people really appreciate painted garage walls and a freshly painted floor leaves a great impression. Make sure the garage doors opener is working and lubricate the hinges and rollers to eliminate any squeaking.

Presenting the Home with Professional Photography

When the home has been prepared, we will be capturing the beauty with professional photography. The objective is to present the home at its best to attract buyers that will be looking online and for use in other marketing materials. A professional architectural photographer will be able to capture the home in the right lighting and the best perspectives so we can tell the story of the home from the exterior and walking into and through the home. The photos should provide an idea of room size and bring the rooms alive. Drone photography is useful to get aerial views if your home is on acreage, you have a pool, or it is a large estate. Matterport tours enable the buyer to walk through the home online.

Special preparation is necessary for the photo shoot to make the home look like a model. It should appear as if no one lives in the home. Of course, the decluttering, staging, and cleaning we have already discussed are all relevant, but we like to go a little further for capturing the very best photos. Everything needs to be freshly cleaned. We want to get as much natural light in all the rooms as possible, so open all window blinds and curtains. Remove small decorative floor rugs so we can showcase flooring. Make sure to remove personal items that you don't want to show up in published photos, such as children's names in bedrooms, family pictures, and confidential information. You should also remove religious or political items and limit holiday or seasonal decorations so the photos will not be dated. Pet items like toys, bowls, beds, and litter boxes should be removed and kennel the pets, if possible.

Go through the entire home and remove any signs of clutter. Remove or straighten books, magazines, or videos on bookshelves. Clear off and organize end tables, dressers, and other furniture. If you have an office, remove stacks of paper and other clutter from the desk. Remove all trashcans and recycling bins. In the kitchen, clear off the countertops and remove any small appliances. Even a coffee pot should be removed for the photos unless it's used for a vignette, even though it might remain during showings later on. Clear all items from refrigerator doors, like photos, magnets, or notes. Of course, dishes should be put away and not left in the sink or on the counters. If closets will be photographed, they should be neat and well organized. In the bathrooms all shampoos, soaps, personal and beauty products need to be put away. Place clean towels neatly folded on the racks. Remove all laundry and laundry baskets throughout the house.

Along with a carefully manicured yard and cleanup, there are some additional preparations for the exterior photos. Vehicles and trailers should be moved from the driveway and away from the front of the house. Open all of the blinds and curtains. Close all of the windows and doors, including the garage door. Remove clutter, like pool toys and cleaning equipment, hoses, garden tools, and sprinklers. Remove the pool cover. For nighttime photo shoots, turn off exterior floodlights and turn on all interior lighting. As discussed earlier, if your home will go on the market during the wintertime, it's better to be able to capture the exterior photos in advance—late summer or autumn—so we can get nice exterior pictures when the yard and exterior look their best.

The above should give a general idea of the detail preparations for shooting photos. I also have an extensive checklist that I give to my clients for more detail so that nothing is missed.

Marketing That Works to Attract Buyers

The photographs are important for all of the marketing channels and platforms we use to attract buyers. Online exposure is critical as most buyers start their home search on the Internet. My listings show on my professional website, the Keller Williams site, and the top real estate sites like Zillow, Realtor.com, and Trulia. Additionally, we syndicate our listing to hundreds of other websites where people are looking for homes. Exposure on social media, such as Facebook, YouTube, and Instagram are also important.

Even with all of the online activity, a high quality printed brochure is always important for people to take away when viewing your home. It really helps them remember the details after they have left and seen other homes on the same day.

Direct mail marketing is something that still works. I like to send out postcards announcing my listing in the community where the home is located. Neighbors may know someone that is interested in buying a home in the area, and that's a good way to get the word out. We also do magazine advertising in publications that are relevant to buyers in the area.

One strategy that I like is "pre-marketing" a property if it's not quite ready for market but will be within a month. We'll show the home on Zillow, which is one of the key sites where we can show the home as "coming soon." This strategy tests the market and when it attracts an offer before the actual listing goes live it is much more likely to get a full-price offer. We can see the interest and possible pent-up demand without additional market days on the MLS (Multiple Listing Service).

Keeping the Home Show-Ready

Your home has been prepared and photographed and now is on the market. You need to be prepared for showings with little notice. Of course, it's going to be difficult, but you should keep everything picked up and as close as possible to the condition when the photos were taken. Again, the home should look as much as possible like you don't live there every day. One practical solution is to keep a couple of laundry baskets in the mud room and you can take the baskets around the house and pick up any clutter, like toys, projects you are working on, mail, and so on and put into the baskets. You can put the baskets in the back of your car when you leave for the showing and bring them back in when you return. No one wants to move into a dirty home, so keeping the home clean, neat and organized is critical.

One of the biggest turn-offs for buyer is the presence of unpleasant odors. Cooking and pet odors are the most common problems. Some sellers decide to cook on their grill outside while their home is on the market to eliminate cooking odors. You can also place air fresheners with a mild, pleasant scent throughout the home. Another idea is to place some cinnamon or other sweet spices on some aluminum foil and warming in the oven to create a pleasant smell.

If you are available at the home before showings, turn on the lights and open the blinds or drapes to get light into the home. If you have a stereo system, you can play some nice classical or jazz music at a low volume to create a nice ambiance. If at all possible, pets should be removed the home during showings.

Selecting an Agent

Your home is a major financial asset and selecting the right agent is critical to obtaining the best outcome for you. One of the most important aspects to look for in an agent is experience and market education in your neighborhood and immediate area as well in overall market conditions and trends. One good indication is the amount of sales they have made and volume of successful transactions. A full-time agent is more likely to provide the attention needed to navigate you all the way through the process to closing. Also look at the online testimonials—what other clients have to say about their experience with the agent. Look at the bio and determine if the agent has awards or other recognition that stands out compared to other agents.

Knowledge of construction details is another important point that not many agents have. The details of each home are different and in order to best represent the seller, the agent should be able to identify the details of the important features, which reflect on the value.

Marketing is a key area to explore. I've talked about the importance of using professional photography to showcase a home. Does the agent use a professional photographer? Are staging services offered, essential in preparing the home? Do they have a list of vendors for home repairs/updates? What is the marketing philosophy and how many different platforms and channels are used to market a home?

Selling a home is a concentrated process and time is of the essence in this business. Determine how the agent will be communicating with you, expectations for answers back, and who you will be communicating with. Also check what resources the agent has available. Does the agent work alone or is there an assistant to help with paperwork?

What Clients Are Saying

"From the initial presentation Kim was professional and knowledgeable of the area and more specifically our home. She was honest and walked us through each step of the way. We have sold and bought many properties in the past and Kim was always on top and ahead of our

questions and concerns. She gave us the confidence needed to entrust in her our listing. Overall it was an awesome process with excellent results."

—Brian and Tanya H.

"Kim is a Woodbury Specialist and the Best! She has assembled a top notch team and they made the process so simple and easy. We had two offers the day we listed at and over asking price."

—Jennifer C.

"We highly recommend Kim Ziton as a realtor. From start to finish of the entire process we always felt Kim had our best interest at heart. She listened to our wants and needs and then helped us sell our old home and also find a new home that was perfect for us. She accompanied us to a meeting with a builder we'd been working with and asked question we hadn't thought of asking. Kim is very knowledgeable with buying an existing home and also with the process of building one. We felt very comfortable in her hands. We really appreciated Kim's professionalism and prompt response time during that difficult time. Kim's assistant Laurie was wonderful to work with too. She always responded quickly to our questions and walked us through things unfamiliar to us. What a great team to work with!"

—Murry and Carol M.

"Here are the things that I believe sets Kim apart from her colleagues: Preparation, timeliness and a tremendous grasp on market knowledge. Her customer service skills are exemplary and she is acutely responsive. Kim uses her vast market knowledge to provide

insightful pricing guidance and will be at her client's side throughout the entire process. Above all these many fine attributes though, my favorite is her professional demeanor. Kim is a pleasure to work with and although I hope I purchased my last home, were I to be a buyer and/or seller, there is absolutely no doubt about whom I would call."

—Bob and Lori P.

"Kim is truly the best in the business. She is extremely knowledgeable about her field and the area. Kim's response time is second to none, and she goes well above and beyond for her clients. Kim helped us find and build our dream home and was an invaluable asset and advocate for us throughout the whole process. We can not say enough positive things about our experience with Kim and HIGHLY recommend her."

—Kevin and Victoria T.

"I had 30 yrs. extensive experience in the mortgage business & Kim was the only realtor open/willing to listen/partner with me on the sale price/details of my home. She included my market value opinions/ research & incorporated it into our listing price. Other prominent local realtors refused to factor my expertise into it which would have resulted in selling for less than purchased in 2005. On purchase/ building side, she attended all meetings & was a key player in all building, exterior/interior selections. Her expertise was exceptional. I highly recommend Kim for truly listening/partnering with me & her expertise on the building side. Couldn't have done it without her!"

—Don and Naomi K.

About Kim Ziton

With 27 years of real estate sales experience, Kim Ziton is a top-producing agent affiliated with Keller Williams Premier Realty's Luxury Homes Division in Woodbury, Minnesota. She has consistently been one of the firm's highest producers and is a member of the Million Dollar Guild. Kim helps buyers and sellers with their real estate transactions in Woodbury and the surrounding eastern suburbs of St. Paul. She holds a real estate license in Minnesota and Wisconsin.

Kim has received a number of awards for sales production including:

- #1 Real Estate Agent in Minnesota and the Region for Keller Williams Premier Realty from 2012 - 2018
- #1 Real Estate Agent in Woodbury for Sales Volume from 2012 - 2018
- #2 Real Estate Agent Worldwide in the Luxury Division for Keller Williams in 2017 – 2018 and #3 in 2016
- In the Top 20 Real Estate Agents Worldwide for Keller Williams Premier Realty in 2015, 2016, and 2017 (out of 139,000 agents)
- Twin Cities Super-Agent by Mpls/St. Paul Magazine from 2011 - 2018
- Voted Best Real Estate Agent in Woodbury 2013 and 2014
- Minneapolis St. Paul Business Journal Book of Lists: Residential Rock Star
- Real Trends America's Best Agents list, which ranks agents' sales by volume in all 50 states

Kim was featured on the cover and in an article in Top Agent Magazine (Minnesota Edition) in 2015, distinguishing her as one of the top real estate professionals in Minnesota.

For more information about Kim Ziton, visit http://www.KimZiton.com.

45932214R00118

Made in the USA
Lexington, KY
20 July 2019